Let's Make

ANGRY BIRDS

CAKES

First published in the United States of America by
Walter Foster, a division of
Quarto Publishing Group USA Inc.
3 Wrigley, Suite A
Irvine, CA 92618
www.walterfoster.com

ISBN: 978-1-58923-856-5

10 9 8 7 6 5 4 3 2 1

Text written by Autumn Carpenter
Photographs by Autumn Carpenter
Copy-edited by Karen Levy
Proofread by Julie Grady
Page layout by Sporto

Printed in China

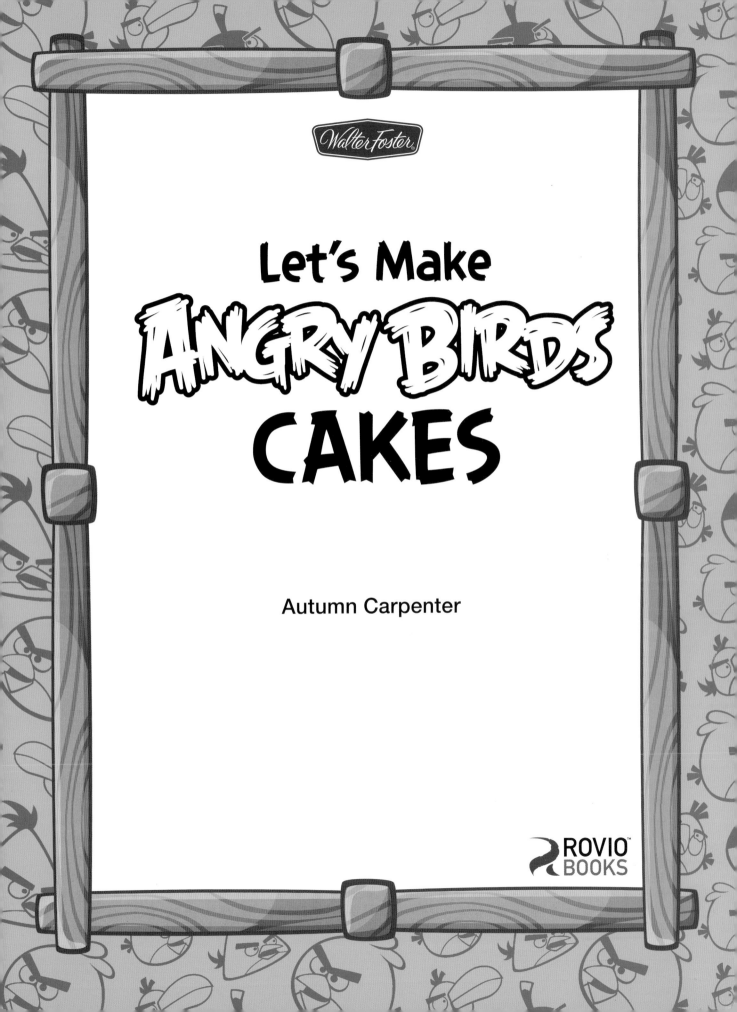

Walter Foster

Let's Make
ANGRY BIRDS
CAKES

Autumn Carpenter

ROVIO BOOKS

CONTENTS

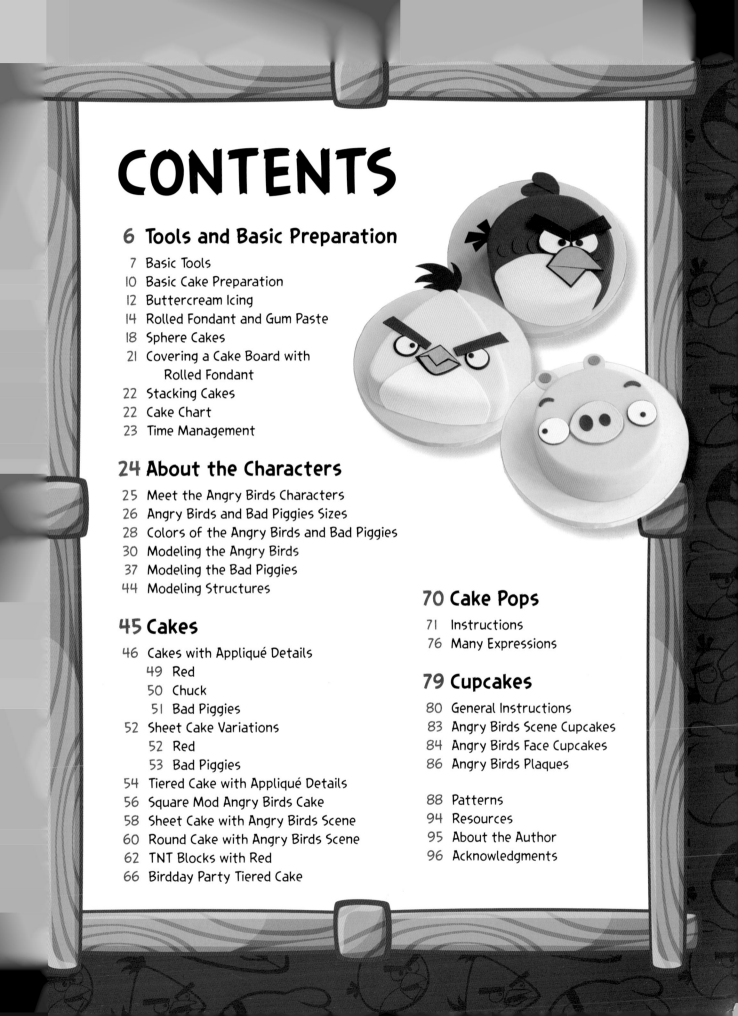

Tools and Basic Preparation

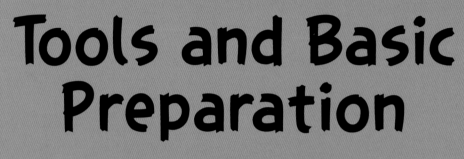

This section covers all the basic tools and decorating equipment needed and instructions for general baking. Next, you'll learn how to bake, ice, and cover a cake with rolled fondant. Discover how to make a three-dimensional sphere for an extraordinary Angry Birds cake. Use the included cake chart to determine how much cake batter, icing, and rolled fondant is needed for the projects. Finally, we'll go over time management tips to ensure you have fun, stress-free baking with your Angry Birds cake projects.

Basic Tools

Before you tackle any of the Angry Birds projects, go through this list of tools to ensure the baking and decorating process goes smoothly. Most of the tools are common essentials for baking and decorating cakes and are likely already in your kitchen.

BAKING TOOLS

Cake Pans

Many of the cake projects use cake or muffin pans that are likely already in your kitchen, including a quarter sheet cake pan and several sizes of round pans. Half-sphere pans are used to create three-dimensional birds and pigs. A convex triangle pan is used for a simple Chuck cake.

Cooling Rack

It is important for cakes to rest on a cooling rack after baking. Cooling racks ensure that the cake will receive even air circulation.

Cake Slicer

Use a cake slicer to make cake layers even.

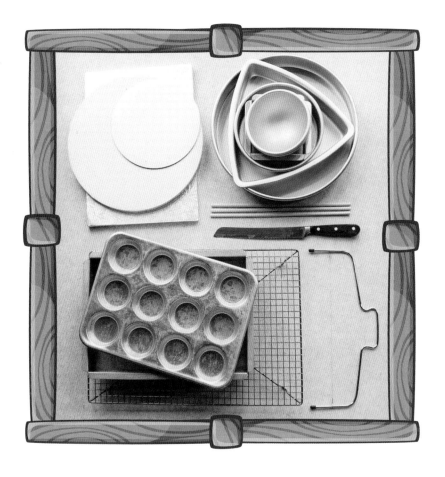

Cake Boards

After your cake is baked, it will need to be placed on a flat, greaseproof cake board. Cake cardboards are fine for small lightweight cakes, but it must be greaseproof or covered in cake foil or a doily. Foil-covered cake drums are ideal. They are lightweight but strong enough to hold a five-tier cake. Cake drums come in several colors, or they can be covered with rolled fondant to coordinate the cake board with the cake.

Dowel Rods

Dowel rods are used to internally support tiered cakes. Without dowels, the cake may become unstable and fall.

DECORATING TOOLS

Fondant Rolling Pin
A nylon white, extra-wide rolling pin (A) is best to use for fondant and gum paste.

Fondant Smoother
Smoothers (B) help give fondant-covered cakes a smooth, satiny finish. Two smoothers should be used, one to keep the cake steady and one to smooth the cake.

Mini Pizza Cutter
When covering a cake, a mini pizza cutter (C) is used to quickly cut excess fondant from around the base. This tool is also ideal for cutting patterns with a straight edge.

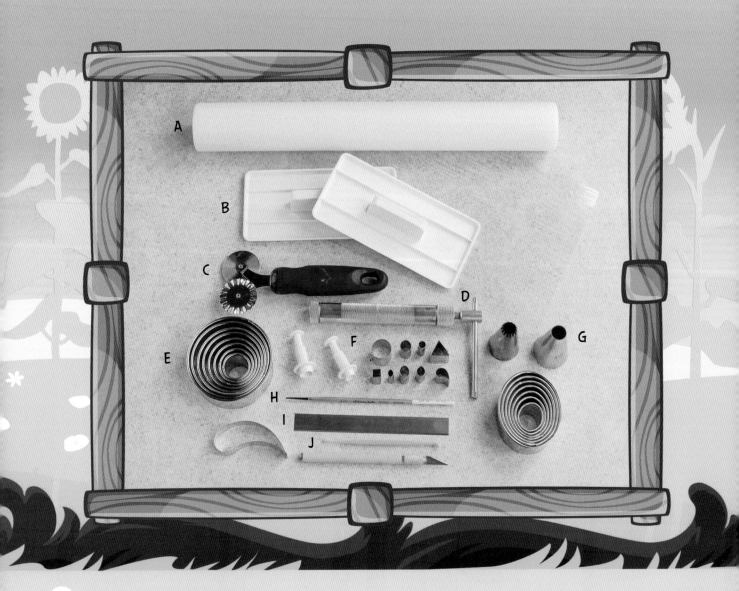

Fondant Extruder

An extruder (D) gives grasslike texture when used with a multi-opening disk.

Cutters

Circle cutters (E) are needed on nearly every project throughout this book. Use a small circle cutter for cutting tiny fondant circles for the eyes on cake pops, or use a larger circle cutter to cut fondant for the top of a cupcake. Keep a wide variety of sizes on hand. The measurements of the circle cutters are given in millimeters for the most accurate sizing. Mini accent cutters (F) are perfect for cutting small facial accents when modeling Angry Birds and Bad Piggies.

Pastry Bags and Piping Tips

Very few pastry tips (G) are used for the Angry Bird treats. Tip #IM is used for piping icing with fine grooves onto a cupcake. Use tip #IA to pipe a round band of icing onto a cupcake. Tip #233 is a fun tip to create a grass texture (see page 12).

Brushes

Use a pastry brush to spread piping gel on large pieces of cut, rolled fondant or onto crusted buttercream before covering a cake with rolled fondant. Brushes with fine bristles (H) are used for painting small details like the ovals on Red. A variety of sizes of brushes are used for brushing small amounts of piping gel when attaching bird and pig details.

Perfection Strips

Use these strips to obtain perfect thickness on your small, rolled accent pieces. A pasta machine is an alternative to perfection strips and is ideal for rolling very thin, small pieces.

Flexible Fondant Blade

Possibly one of the most useful tools (I), it is used on nearly every project. Its thin, stainless, steel blade cuts a straight sharp edge. The flexible blade allows you to easily cut free flowing shapes. Use the blade to cut nice straight lines for bird eyebrows and head feathers. It is also used to trim excess fondant away when covering cake boards.

Modeling Tools

A modeling tool with a ball on the end (J) is used to create crevices for pig ears and indentations in the pig nostrils.

Toothpicks

Toothpicks are used to assemble and support structures.

Icing Spatulas

A spatula with a long blade is used to spread buttercream icing on the cake. A spatula with a shorter blade is used to mix small amounts of icing and to spread the icing on the sides of the cake.

Basic Cake Preparation

There are many books devoted to cake recipes and hundreds of recipes online, many of which are complete with ratings and baking suggestions. For those who want to bake a cake quickly, commercial manufacturers of cake mixes have done a fantastic job perfecting their mixes. Most cakes in this book adapt well to your favorite recipe. For creating any of the cakes in a sphere shape, use a dense cake, such as pound cake, for stability.

BAKING ROUND, SQUARE, AND SHEET CAKES

1. Preheat the oven according to the recipe's instructions. Using a pastry brush, generously spread pan grease thoroughly in the pan. Pan grease is available at cake and candy supply stores. If pan grease is unavailable, thoroughly spread solid vegetable shortening in the pan, and then dust with all-purpose flour. Prepare the cake batter according to the recipe's instructions. Pour the batter into the cake pan, filling the pan just over half full.

2. Place the filled pan in the oven and bake according to the recipe's instructions. Check to see if the cake is done by inserting a cake tester into the center of the cake. If the cake tester comes out clean or with a few cake crumbs, the cake is done. If the tester comes out with batter, the cake is not thoroughly baked. Leave the cake in the oven and test again after a minute or two.

LEVELING ROUND, SQUARE, AND SHEET CAKES

3. After the cake is baked, remove the pan from the oven and place the pan on a cooling rack. Allow the cake to cool in the pan for 10 minutes.

4. After cooling for 10 minutes, run a knife along the edge of the pan to loosen the sides. When the pan is cool enough to handle, place a second cooling rack on top of the cake pan, sandwiching the pan between the cooling racks. Hold on to the two cooling racks tightly and flip over the pan. Place the cooling racks on the counter and remove the top cooling rack. Gently lift the cake pan. Allow the cake to cool completely before decorating, or the icing will melt. If the cake is domed, use a cake slicer to level the top.

SANDWICHING TWO LAYER CAKES

5. Fit a pastry bag with tip #2A. Fill the bag with buttercream icing. Pipe a ring of icing around the edge of the cake, leaving approximately 1/2 inch (1.3 cm) of space from the edge. Continue piping rings, working your way to the center.

6. Spread the icing to smooth, nearly to the edge.

7. Center the second layer on top of the first.

Buttercream Icing

The cakes throughout this book are covered with rolled fondant, which gives a clean, smooth finish. To add extra sweetness, the cake may be iced with buttercream, then covered with rolled fondant. Buttercream provides stickiness for the rolled fondant to attach to the cake. A turntable makes icing round and sphere cakes easier while allowing the icing to be spread more evenly on the sides. The included buttercream recipe will crust on the outside. If the buttercream crusts before covering the cake with rolled fondant, a layer of piping gel should be brushed on top of the buttercream for the rolled fondant to adhere.

BUTTERCREAM VS. FONDANT

Many of the cakes throughout the book adapt well if you prefer a cake covered with buttercream instead of rolled fondant. Accents should still be made in rolled fondant or gum paste, but the cake can be iced in buttercream. For example, this cake is the same design as the fondant-covered cake on page 58, but this one is iced in buttercream.

Tip #233 has multiple round openings and is ideal for piping grass with buttercream.

Buttercream Icing Recipe

½ cup (112 g) high-ratio shortening
4 cups (480 g) powdered sugar, sifted
5 tablespoons (75 ml) water
½ teaspoon (2.5 mL) salt
1 teaspoon (5 mL) vanilla flavoring
½ teaspoon (2.5 mL) almond flavoring
¼ teaspoon (1.5 mL) butter flavoring

1. In a large bowl, combine all the ingredients; beat on low speed until well blended. Continue beating on low speed for 10 minutes, or until very creamy. Keep the bowl covered to prevent the icing from drying out. Unused icing can be kept in the refrigerator for up to 6 weeks. Rewhip on low speed before piping.

Yields 4 cups (1 L)

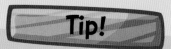

Tip!

- For bright white icing, use clear flavorings. Pure vanilla will give the icing an ivory hue.
- Solid vegetable shortening can be substituted for high-ratio shortening, which is a baker's quality product intended to replace butter in icing and cake recipes. High-ratio shortening gives the icing a fine, smooth, and creamy texture without a greasy aftertaste. Solid vegetable shortening will likely affect the icing consistency, texture, and flavor.
- Whipping the buttercream on low speed creates a smooth, creamy icing. Whipping on medium or high speed will create air bubbles.

ICING A CAKE WITH BUTTERCREAM

1. If the cake will be covered with fondant, place the cake on a cake cardboard the same size as the cake. While icing, ice the edges of the cardboard as though it is part of the cake. If the cake will not be covered in fondant, the cake can be iced directly on the serving board. Mix a small amount of icing with water to thin the buttercream. When spread, you should just barely see crumbs underneath. Spread the thinned icing on the cake to form a crumb coat. Allow the crumb coat to form a crust (usually 20 to 45 minutes).

2. After the crumb coat has set, place a generous amount of icing on top of the cake. With a long spatula, spread the icing on the top using long strokes and gliding toward the edge.

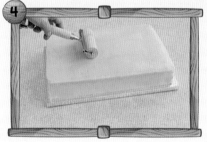

3. Apply icing to the side of the cake. Hold a smaller spatula perpendicular to the cake when spreading the icing on the sides. Blend the icing from the top with the icing on the sides. Glide the spatula along the top and sides of the cake to smooth.

4. After the icing forms a crust (approximately 45 minutes), gently roll over any areas that are not smooth with a pastry roller.

Rolled Fondant and Gum Paste

ROLLED FONDANT

Rolled fondant is used to cover cakes and to create accents on cakes, cupcakes, and cake pops. The icing has a chewy texture and a sweet, vanilla flavor. It is available commercially in white and in many colors; many are close matches to the Angry Birds colors. Before covering a cake with fondant, the cake should have an under-icing. Icing the cake first in buttercream gives the cake a smooth base while adding sweetness and sealing in moisture. A recipe for rolled fondant is included. It can be difficult to obtain the proper texture, so before attempting the recipe, purchase commercial rolled fondant to become familiar with the texture and consistency. Rolled fondant will dry out quickly, so keep it tightly wrapped and sealed when not in use.

Rolled Fondant Recipe

½ cup (120 mL) cream
2 tablespoons (16 g) unflavored gelatin
¾ cup (175 mL) glucose
2 tablespoons (28 g) unsalted butter
2 tablespoons (25 ml) glycerin
2 teaspoons (10 mL) clear vanilla flavor
2 teaspoons (10 mL) clear butter flavor
1 teaspoon (5 mL) clear almond flavor
Approximately 9 cups (1 kg) powdered sugar
Vegetable shortening

1. Pour the cream into a small saucepan. Sprinkle the gelatin on the cream and cook over low heat until the gelatin is dissolved. Add the glucose, butter, glycerin, and flavorings. Heat until the butter is melted. Set aside.

2. Sift the powdered sugar. Place 7 cups (770 g) of the powdered sugar in the bowl of a stand mixer fitted with the dough hook attachment. Pour the cream mixture over the powdered sugar and mix slowly until the powdered sugar is thoroughly mixed. Add the remaining 2 cups (220 g) powdered sugar. The fondant will be very sticky, but should hold its shape.

3. Lay a sheet of plastic wrap on the counter. Coat with a thin layer of vegetable shortening. Wrap the fondant in the greased plastic wrap and allow it to set for 24 hours. After 24 hours, the fondant should be less sticky. If not, add more powdered sugar.

GUM PASTE

Gum paste is used to make accents that are stronger, firmer, and more detailed than rolled fondant. Gum paste sets very hard and should not be eaten. It is best for hand molding the Angry Bird characters and, most importantly, the Angry Bird structures (page 44). Gum paste can be made from scratch. Included is a recipe from Nicholas Lodge, an excellent cake decorator and teacher known for his unique, intricate sugar work. Gum paste can also be purchased commercially or made by adding food-grade tylose to rolled fondant. Add approximately 1 tablespoon (15 ml) of tylose to 1 pound (454 g) of rolled fondant. Allow the tylose fondant to sit for a few hours before shaping.

Tip!

· Gum paste dries out quickly. Add less tylose if more working time is desired. Wrap tightly when not in use. When gum paste is overworked, it will become stiff and toughen. A touch of shortening or egg whites can be added to soften the paste.

Nicholas Lodge's Gum Paste Recipe

4 ³/₈ ounces (125 g) fresh egg whites
2 pounds 2 ounces (950 g) powdered sugar
Food coloring (optional)
1 ¼ ounces (35 g) tylose powder
³/₄ ounce (20g) solid vegetable shortening

1. Place the egg whites in the bowl of a stand mixer fitted with the flat paddle. Turn the mixer on high speed for 10 seconds to break up the egg whites.

2. Turn the mixer to the lowest speed; slowly add 1 pound 9 ounces (700 g) of the powdered sugar. This will make a soft consistency royal icing. Turn up the speed to setting 3 or 4 for about 2 minutes. Make sure the mixture is at the soft-peak stage. It should look shiny, like meringue, and the peaks should fall over. If coloring the whole batch, add the paste or gel food color at this stage, making it a shade darker than the desired color.

3. Turn the mixer to the low setting and sprinkle the tylose in over a 5-second time period. Turn the speed up to the high setting for a few seconds. This will thicken the mixture.

4. Scrape the mixture out of the bowl onto a work surface that has been sprinkled with some of the remaining 9 ounces (250 g) powdered sugar. Rub the shortening on your hands and knead the paste, adding enough of the reserved powdered sugar to form soft, but not sticky dough. Check the consistency by pinching the dough with your fingers. Your fingers should come away clean.

5. Place the finished paste in a zip-top bag, then place the bagged paste in a second bag and seal well. Allow the gum paste to mature for 24 hours before use, keeping it in a cool environment. When ready to use the paste, cut off a small amount and knead a little vegetable shortening into the paste. If coloring at this stage, knead the color into the paste until the desired shade is achieved. When not in use, the paste will need to be stored in the refrigerator. Always store the paste in doubled zip-top bags. The paste will keep in the refrigerator for approximately 6 months.

Rolled Fondant and Gum Paste

COVERING A CAKE WITH ROLLED FONDANT

A cake covered in rolled fondant has a smooth, clean appearance. An under-icing of buttercream gives extra sweetness and helps the fondant stick to the cake. Placing the cake on a cardboard the same size (not larger) as the cake allows you to easily move it after it is covered. Work quickly through the entire fondant-covering process; try to complete all the steps within 5 to 7 minutes. The fondant may develop tiny cracks or "elephant skin" if too much time has elapsed. When rolling fondant, it is important to rotate to ensure the fondant maintains an even shape. However, do not flip the fondant over, as residue from the countertop will stick to the fondant and be unsightly.

1. Bake and cool the cake. Place the cake on a cardboard the same size. With buttercream, crumb coat the cake, then ice the cake following instructions on page 13. If the buttercream has crusted, brush the iced cake with piping gel.

2. Dust the work surface with powdered sugar. Knead and soften the rolled fondant. Roll the fondant, lifting and turning the fondant every other roll. If the fondant is sticking to the surface, add more powdered sugar. Do not flip the rolled fondant over. Continue rolling until the fondant is approximately ⅛" (3 mm) thick and the diameter of the cake plus the height of the cake doubled plus at least 4" (10 cm) to allow for placement if the fondant is not perfectly centered. For example, the cake that is shown is 8" (20.3 cm) in diameter and 4" (10.2 cm) tall. Therefore, the final diameter of the fondant should be at least 20" (50.8 cm). Lift the rolled fondant using the rolling pin. Start at the base of the cake and unroll the fondant onto the cake.

3. Lift and shift the sides to eliminate any creases. Take care not to stretch and pull the fondant.

4. Secure the edges by pressing your palms against the sides of the cake.

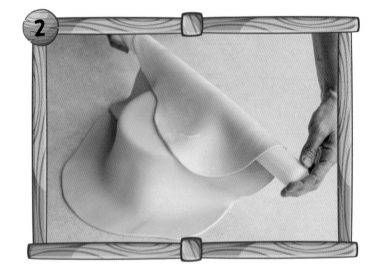

5. With a mini pizza cutter, cut excess fondant, leaving about 1" (2.5 cm) all around the base.

6. Lay the pizza cutter nearly perpendicular to the work surface and trim under the cake, leaving a clean, finished edge at the bottom.

7. With your nondominant hand, rest one fondant smoother on the top of the cake to hold the cake steady and to smooth the top. Do not apply pressure or the smoother will impress lines. Smooth the sides with another fondant smoother.

8. Spread buttercream on a cake plate or cake cardboard. Lift the cake using a jumbo spatula and place on the cake plate.

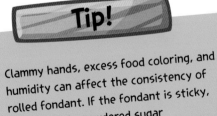

Tip!

Clammy hands, excess food coloring, and humidity can affect the consistency of rolled fondant. If the fondant is sticky, knead a little powdered sugar into it.

Sphere Cakes

BAKING, ICING, AND COVERING WITH ROLLED FONDANT

The Angry Birds cake on page 62 use a 5" (12.5 cm) sphere pan. This size is ideal for beginners and looks quite nice on sheet cakes or on top of a tiered cake. You can also make Angry Birds or Bad Piggies cakes using other sizes of sphere pans. When creating sphere cakes, a dense cake recipe, such as pound cake, is best to use for extra stability.

Baking, icing, and covering a sphere with rolled fondant can be tricky. When baking, be sure to fill the pan nearly to the top to ensure the cake will rise properly. When covering the cake with icing, it is much easier to pipe the icing onto the cake using a pastry bag and then spread the icing rather than simply spreading icing directly from a bowl. When covering the sphere with fondant, it is important to roll extra fondant so you'll have plenty to work with when covering the cake.

1. Preheat the oven according to the recipe's instructions. Using a pastry brush, generously spread pan grease thoroughly in the sphere pans. If pan grease is unavailable, thoroughly spread solid vegetable shortening in the pans, and then dust with all-purpose flour. If the pans did not come with rings or bottom supports to keep the bowls from rolling, create rings using aluminum foil. Place the pans and bottom supports on a cookie sheet.

2. Prepare the dense cake batter according to the recipe's instructions. Pour the batter into the cake pans, filling the pans just over three-fourths full to ensure the cake will rise over the top of the pans. Place the filled pans in the oven and bake according to the recipe's instructions. Check to see if the cakes are done by inserting a cake tester into the center of the cakes. If the cake tester comes out clean or with a few cake crumbs, the cakes are done. If the tester comes out with batter, the cakes are not thoroughly baked. Leave the cakes in the oven and test again after a minute or two.

3. After the cakes are baked, remove them from the oven and place the cookie sheet containing the sphere cakes on a cooling rack. Allow the cakes to cool in the pan for 10 minutes. Use a knife to loosen the edges between the cake and the pan. While the cakes are still in the pans, use a serrated knife to level.

4. After cooling for 20 minutes and leveling the top, remove the half spheres and place directly on the cooling rack. Allow the cakes to cool completely. Slice a small sliver off the top on one half sphere. This is for the bottom of the sphere and will create a flat surface so the sphere does not roll.

5. Cut a greaseproof board in a 2 ½" (6.4 cm) circle. Pipe buttercream icing onto the board to secure the sphere.

6. Place the half sphere cake on the board, cut edge down. Pipe an even layer of buttercream to sandwich the two half spheres.

7. Using tip #2A, generously pipe buttercream on the sphere cake until it is nearly covered.

(continued)

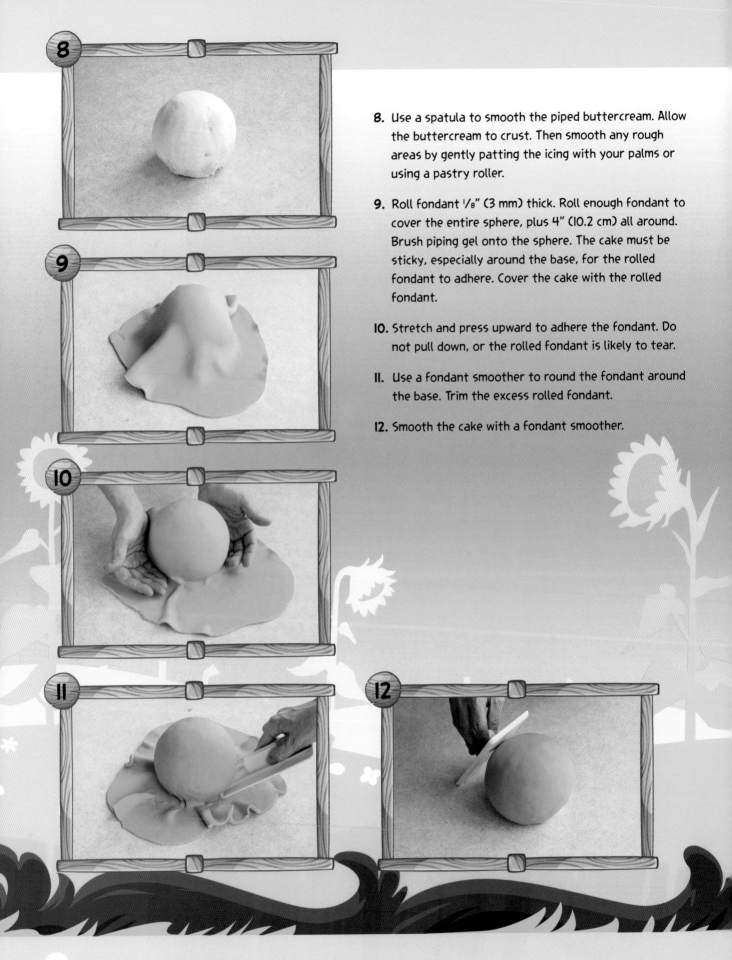

8. Use a spatula to smooth the piped buttercream. Allow the buttercream to crust. Then smooth any rough areas by gently patting the icing with your palms or using a pastry roller.

9. Roll fondant ⅛" (3 mm) thick. Roll enough fondant to cover the entire sphere, plus 4" (10.2 cm) all around. Brush piping gel onto the sphere. The cake must be sticky, especially around the base, for the rolled fondant to adhere. Cover the cake with the rolled fondant.

10. Stretch and press upward to adhere the fondant. Do not pull down, or the rolled fondant is likely to tear.

11. Use a fondant smoother to round the fondant around the base. Trim the excess rolled fondant.

12. Smooth the cake with a fondant smoother.

Covering a Cake Board with Rolled Fondant

Covering a cake board with rolled fondant harmonizes the design of the cake from top to bottom. Cover the cake board a few days ahead of time to allow the fondant to harden, so it will not become damaged when setting the cake on the board.

CAKE BOARD WITH A SMOOTH FINISH

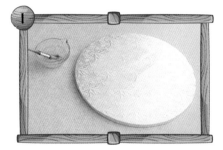  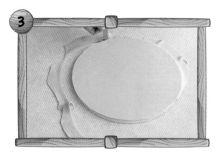

1. Brush piping gel over the entire surface of the cake board.

2. Knead and soften the fondant. Dust the work surface with powdered sugar. Roll the fondant until it is approximately 1/8" (3 mm) thick. Make sure enough fondant is rolled to fit the diameter of the cake board. Place the rolled fondant on the piping gel-covered board. Glide over the board with fondant smoothers to flatten and remove any air pockets.

3. Holding a flexible fondant blade perpendicular to the board, cut off excess fondant. If desired, attach ribbon to the edge of the board using fabric glue.

CAKE BOARD WITH A TEXTURED FINISH

1. Knead and soften the fondant. Roll the fondant until it is approximately 1/8" (3 mm) thick. Place the clean, smooth side of the fondant face down onto a texture mat. Starting on one side of the fondant, using a lot of pressure, roll the fondant in one direction. Do not roll back and forth, or double lines will result.

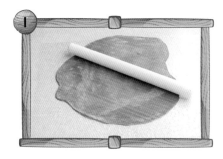

2. Brush piping gel over the entire surface of the cake board. Lift the mat and position the mat on the piping gel-coated cake board. Peel back the texture mat. Holding a flexible fondant blade perpendicular to the board, cut off excess fondant. If desired, attach ribbon to the edge of the board using fabric glue.

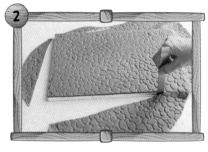

Stacking Cakes

It's important to properly stack cakes or they may fall. Cakes should not be stacked on top of one another without support. Choose plastic plates or cake boards that are grease-resistant. Plain cardboard that is not covered will absorb grease and the cardboard may become unstable. The dowels shown are ¼" (6 mm) in diameter, but other sizes can be used. When cutting the dowels, make sure they are cut to the height of the icing and not any higher. If there is extra height, the cake may have a gap in between the tiers. Note that 14" (35.6 cm) or larger tiers should have additional dowels and at least one in the center.

1. Spread some icing on a sturdy base plate. Place the bottom tier on the base plate. The remaining tiers should be placed on a plastic plate or a grease-resistant plate that is the same size as the cake. Place a cake plate, the same size as the top tier, on the cake to determine where the dowels will be inserted. For the example shown, the cake will be placed toward the back of the cake and not centered. Use a toothpick to mark around the plate.

2. Remove the plate. Insert one dowel into the iced cake. The dowel should be approximately ½" (1.3 cm) from the edge of the tier that will be placed on top. Mark the height of the cake. Remove the dowel. With a hacksaw, cut four dowels the same height as the marked dowel. Place the dowels back into the cake after they have been cut.

3. Spread a layer of icing in the center of the marked area. Place the top layer on the cake.

Cake Chart

Numbers and amounts for a sheet cake are based on a one-layer cake; for round and square cakes they are based on two-layer cakes. The number of servings will depend entirely on how large or how small the cake is cut. When figuring the size of cake to bake, bigger is better. It is better to err with extra cake than to run out of cake.

One standard cake mix contains four to six cups (1 to 1.5 L) of batter. The charts for the amount of batter needed are based on a single pan that is 2" (5 cm) tall, filling ⅔ full with cake batter. If the pan is less than ⅔ full, the cake will likely be too thin.

The amount of icing needed is based on icing the cake with the buttercream icing recipe included in this book. The amount of icing needed will vary according to the consistency, thickness applied, or if other recipes are used.

The figures for the amount of icing needed include enough icing for piping a border or simple piped accents. The figure for the amount of fondant needed includes just the amount needed for covering the cake and does not include additional decorations. This amount can vary significantly depending on the thickness of the rolled fondant.

SHEET CAKES	NUMBER OF SERVINGS	CAKE BATTER NEEDED	ICING NEEDED	FONDANT NEEDED	BAKE TEMP	BAKE TIME
9" x 13" (23 x 33 cm) (quarter sheet cake)	20	6 cups (1.5 L)	6 cups (1.5 L)	40 ounces (1 kg)	350°F (175°C)	35-40 min
ROUND CAKES	**NUMBER OF SERVINGS**	**CAKE BATTER NEEDED**	**ICING NEEDED**	**FONDANT NEEDED**	**BAKE TEMP**	**BAKE TIME**
6" (15 cm)	8	1¼ cups (300 mL)	3 cups (750 mL)	18 ounces (0.5 kg)	350°F (175°C)	25-30 min
8" (20 cm)	18	2½ cups (625 mL)	4½ cups (1.125 L)	24 ounces (0.7 kg)	350°F (175°C)	30-35 min
10" (25 cm)	28	4¼ cups (1 L)	5½ cups (1.375 L)	36 ounces (1 kg)	350°F (175°C)	35-40 min
12" (30 cm)	40	5½ cups (1.4 L)	6½ cups (1.6 L)	48 ounces (1.3 kg)	350°F (175°C)	35-40 min
14" (36 cm)	64	7½ cups (1.8 L)	7¾ cups (1.9 L)	72 ounces (2 kg)	325°F (160°C)	50-55 min
SQUARE CAKES	**NUMBER OF SERVINGS**	**CAKE BATTER NEEDED**	**ICING NEEDED**	**FONDANT NEEDED**	**BAKE TEMP**	**BAKE TIME**
6" (15 cm)	12	2¼ cups (550 mL)	4 cups (1 L)	24 ounces (0.7 kg)	350°F (175°C)	25-30 min
8" (20 cm)	22	4 cups (1 L)	5 cups (1.25 L)	36 ounces (1 kg)	350°F (175°C)	35-40 min
10" (25 cm)	35	7 cups (1.75 L)	6½ cups (1.6 L)	48 ounces (1.3 kg)	350°F (175°C)	35-40 min

Time Management

The cake and cupcake projects vary in level of difficulty as well as the amount of time needed to complete them. Some of the projects, such as the Angry Birds sheet cake faces, are simple and can be made in a few hours, while others may take many hours to complete. Do not wait until the day before the party to take on these projects. With well-thought-out planning, you can create these elaborate cakes without stress. The shelf life and storage of the cakes will vary according to the recipe used. This general timeline is for baked cakes that taste best when eaten within 3 days. Rolled fondant and gum paste decorations for most projects can and should be made ahead. Use the following chart as a suggested time line.

ONE MONTH PRIOR	Plan the design. Compile a shopping list and purchase supplies online or shop at your local cake store. Write a time line with tasks to complete. Print the patterns needed, resizing if necessary.
TEN DAYS PRIOR	Cover the cake board with rolled fondant. Make any gum paste pieces that need to be firm. Create any rolled fondant accents. Store gum paste and fondant pieces in a dry area at room temperature. Do not put the pieces in an airtight container or they will not harden.
FIVE DAYS PRIOR	If making icing from scratch, prepare it. Store according to the recipe directions.
TWO DAYS PRIOR	Bake the cake or cupcakes. Ice the cake or cupcakes. Cover the cake or cupcakes with fondant.
DAY OF THE PARTY	Add the decorations or accents to the cake. Enjoy your fantastic work of art!

About the Characters

This section introduces you to the phenomenal Angry Birds and Bad Piggies. Begin by learning about their distinct personalities. Next, study their sizes and colors to ensure all the characters look authentic when created for your cakes. After that, you are ready to hand mold and sculpt the characters. This section includes step-by-step instructions for creating the Angry Birds characters and structures in rolled fondant or gum paste. With this knowledge, you can easily duplicate the Angry Birds scenes in this book, or be inspired to create your own Angry Birds scene.

Learning about each of the Angry Birds and Bad Piggies personalities will help when designing your own cakes. Study their faces, carefully observing their features. The position of the features is the most important factor for accuracy. For example, the Bad Piggies' eyes are centered beside the nose, not above.

RED

Red is the Angry Bird—the leader and angriest of all the birds. He protects the eggs at all costs.

CHUCK

Chuck is Red's loyal friend and the fastest of the birds. Chuck acts before he thinks, and this often lands him in trouble.

BOMB

Bomb is able to explode at will and just loves to blow things up. However, he is not fully in control of his powers.

MATILDA

Matilda loves nature and tries to find peaceful solutions to problems. She loses her peaceful mind-set completely when she snaps.

HAL

Hal is an adventurer bird who enjoys playing his banjo on the sunny side of the island.

TERENCE

The pigs find Terence very frightening. No one knows what goes on in his head because he almost never speaks.

THE BLUES

The Blues—Jim, Jake, and Jay—are the youngest of the birds. They like to play pranks and are sometimes a bit irresponsible.

MINION PIGS

The Minion Pigs are doing their best to find eggs for their King. They are the lowest of the low in the pig society, but are still generally happy with their lives.

CORPORAL PIG

Corporal Pig is the loyal leader of the King's army. He tirelessly leads his troops from failure to failure.

FOREMAN PIG

Foreman Pig supervises the building of all the pigs' contraptions. He is very self-confident, but incompetent.

KING PIG

King Pig is the leader of the pigs and the only pig who is allowed to eat eggs. His big secret is that he doesn't have any eggs in his treasure chamber.

If several Angry Birds and Bad Piggies will be included on the cake or cupcakes, use this chart as a guideline to create the most accurate representation for the size of the characters.

RED

Red's eyes are centered on his body. His belly rests just below his eyes with a little bit of space between. Red's beak rests on top of his eyes and part of his belly.

THE BLUES

The Blues are smaller than Red and they don't share the characteristic eyebrows of the Angry Birds.

CHUCK

Chuck's signature triangle shape makes him stand out from all the other birds. His white belly is at the bottom third of his body. His eyebrows rest in the middle of his triangle body. The beak is positioned half on the white of his belly.

BOMB

Bomb is larger than Red. The bottom of his beak rests just above the center of his body. The eyes are on the upper quarter of the body. The single head feather boasts an orange tip that matches his beak.

MINION PIGS

There are several sizes of these cheeky pigs. The smallest Minion Pig is slightly smaller than Red, but larger than The Blues.

CORPORAL PIG

The Corporal Pig is bulkier than the Minion Pigs and wears a helmet of steel. He is in between the Minion Pigs and Foreman Pig in size.

TERENCE

Terence is bigger, wrinklier, and grumpier than Red. Notice how the head comb and his pupils are about the same size as Red's. His eyebrows are thick and cover a bit more of his eyes compared with Red.

HAL

Hal's massive beak is about a third the size of his head. Hal's body is slightly smaller than Red's, but his head feathers make him just as tall.

MATILDA

Egg-laying Matilda is an egg shape size in between Red and Bomb. Her short, strong beak takes up a good portion of her body. Her oval cheeks are a light green.

FOREMAN PIG

Forman Pig sits almost as large as King Pig and sports bright orange eyebrows and a bright orange moustache.

KING PIG

King Pig stands out from the others by his massive size and the crown atop his head.

Use these suggested colors when coloring buttercream or kneading color into rolled fondant and gum paste. Keep in mind that these are just suggestions, as manufacturers of food coloring and rolled fondant may use the same names, but the hues may vary. Choose concentrated gels and pastes when coloring. Liquid coloring will not give vibrant tints. If coloring buttercream, squeeze the color into the icing and stir with a spatula. Buttercream icing tends to darken as it sits, so allow the icing to sit for a couple of hours before icing the cake to ensure the color is as desired. When coloring fondant, squeeze the color onto the fondant and knead in the color until no streaks appear. For convenience, rolled fondant comes already colored from several manufacturers and in many cases is very close to the Angry Birds colors.

Beaks

The birds' beaks are not bright orange, but rather yellow-orange in color. Start with yellow icing or fondant. Add a few drops of orange color.

Red and Black Colors

It can be tricky to obtain a nice, bright red or a true black. Too much red or black color in buttercream may cause the icing to taste bitter. Too much coloring in fondant may cause the fondant to become sticky. Fondant can be purchased commercially in a beautiful bright red and a wonderful black. There are no-taste red food colorings available, though most do not produce vivid color. Get the icing as red as possible, then add super red food coloring to brighten the no-taste red buttercream.

For black icing, first add cocoa powder to obtain a dark chocolate icing, then add the black coloring. The cocoa powder may cause the buttercream to stiffen. Add a small amount of water to achieve the desired consistency.

Terra-Cotta

Terra-cotta is used for Chuck's eyebrows, Bomb's eyebrows, and The Blues' eyelids. Many manufacturers have a terra-cotta color. Copper is also close in color to terra-cotta. If terra-cotta or copper cannot be found, start with orange and add a touch of brown food coloring.

Burgundy

Burgundy is used on Red's cheeks. Many manufacturers have a burgundy or maroon color. If burgundy cannot be found, start with red and add a small amount of pink, and then a tiny amount of blue and brown.

Ivory

Red and Matilda have ivory bellies. If ivory cannot be found, start with white and add a small amount of brown. If the ivory looks too pink, add a tiny drop of green. If the ivory looks too green, add a tiny drop of pink.

Gray

Bomb has gray on his belly and eyelids. Gray is made by simply starting with white icing or fondant and adding a touch of black.

The Blues

These birds appear bright blue, but add a touch of pink to the blue to give them their characteristic color.

Bad Piggies

The Bad Piggies' features contain several shades of green. Most of them start with leaf green, and then are modified. Make a dark leaf green and add a couple drops of black to obtain the dark green for the eyebrows and nostrils. Start with yellow for the nose, then add a couple drops of leaf green.

- Super Red
- Super Black
- Burgundy
- Yellow-Orange
- Ivory

- Super Black
- Leaf Green
- Yellow Orange

- Royal Blue with a touch of Pink
- Super Black
- Terra-Cotta
- Yellow Orange

- Leaf Green
- Leaf Green with a touch of Black
- Yellow with a touch of Leaf Green
- Leaf Green with a touch of Yellow

- Super Black
- Lemon Yellow
- Terra-Cotta
- Yellow Orange

- Terra-Cotta
- Super Black
- Yellow Orange
- Grey

- Super Black
- Yellow with a touch of Green
- Yellow Orange
- Ivory

The following instructions are for creating hand-molded Angry Birds. These figures can be made several weeks ahead. Keep the figures in a loosely covered box. Expand your creativity and hand mold characters with several expressions. For more Angry Birds expressions, see the cake pops on pages 70-78.

SHAPING THE BODIES

Before making the Angry Birds' bodies, insert toothpicks into Styrofoam. The toothpicks should extend out of the Styrofoam to nearly the height, but not any taller, than the bird that will be made. All of the Angry Birds' bodies start with a round shape. Matilda is made by forming a ball, then shaping the ball into an egg. Chuck is made by forming a ball, then shaping the ball into a triangle. It's best to shape the bodies, and then allow the bodies to harden overnight to avoid misshaping them when adding the features. Form the Angry Birds' bodies and place them on the toothpick.
Use the chart on pages 26-27 for guidelines when sizing the bodies.

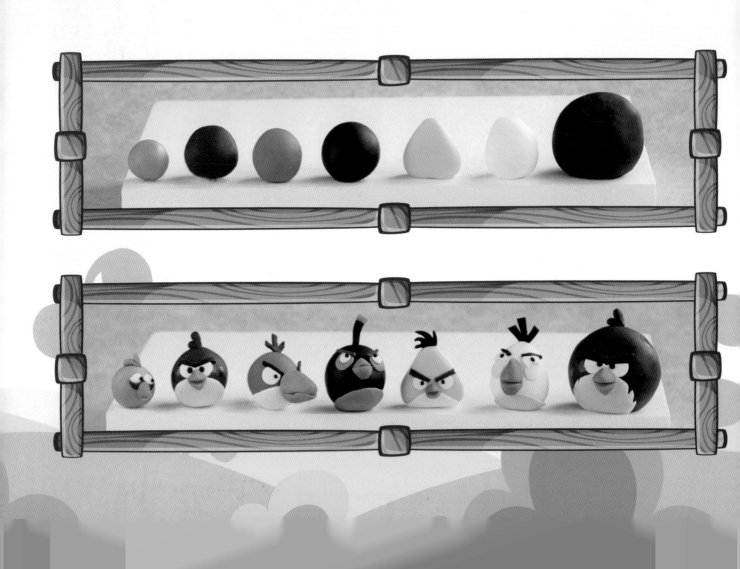

CUTTING THE EYEBROWS

All of the Angry Birds except The Blues have long, rectangular eyebrows. Roll the fondant thin. Cut strips using a flexible fondant blade. Cut the strip into pieces for individual eyebrows.

CUTTING THE HEAD AND TAIL FEATHERS

The head feathers vary in shape and design. Red, Terence, and The Blues have head feathers that are hand-molded teardrops. The other birds have head feathers that are cut. To cut the head feathers and tail feathers, roll the fondant thin. Cut the general shape of the head feathers using a flexible fondant blade. Then, cut the details using the same fondant blade, bending the blade if necessary to achieve the curved parts, such as Chuck's head feathers.

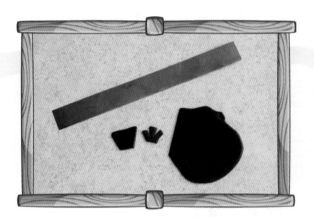

SHAPING AND CUTTING THE BEAKS

All of the beaks, except Hal's, are created the same way: form a ball, shape the ball into a cone, then cut the beak with a flexible fondant blade to separate it into two parts. Cut straight down into the beak, stopping about three-fourths of the way. Study the birds' beaks on pages 26-27. Note the position of the two beak parts. Some of the birds' beaks are cut in the bottom third, including Red, The Blues, Chuck, Matilda, and Terence. The beak is larger on the top and smaller on the bottom. Bomb's beak should be cut in the upper third, making it smaller at the top and larger on the bottom.

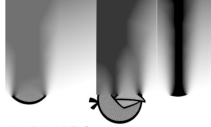

THE BLUES

Blue rolled fondant
Terra-cotta rolled fondant
White rolled fondant
Black rolled fondant
Orange rolled fondant
Piping gel
Oval cutter, 13 mm
Flexible fondant blade

1. Knead and soften the blue rolled fondant. Roll a ball for the bird's body. Place the ball into a toothpick set in Styrofoam. Allow the body to harden overnight.

2. Knead and soften the terra-cotta rolled fondant. Roll thin. Cut two ovals using the 13 mm oval cutter. Cut off the bottom fourth of each oval using the same cutter.

3. Knead and soften the white rolled fondant. Roll thin. Cut two ovals using the 13 mm oval cutter. Cut off the bottom fifth of each oval.

4. Knead and soften the black rolled fondant. Roll two small black balls for the pupils. Attach the pupils to the white eyes using piping gel.

5. Knead and soften the blue rolled fondant. Roll two teardrops, making one a little larger than the other.

6. Knead and soften the orange rolled fondant. Form and cut the beak.

7. Add the birds' features, using piping gel as the glue. First, attach the terra-cotta ovals, then the eyes. Attach the beak. Finally, add the two blue teardrops.

RED

Red rolled fondant
Ivory rolled fondant
White rolled fondant
Black rolled fondant
Orange rolled fondant
Piping gel
Burgundy food coloring
Round cutter, 13 mm
Round cutter, 30 mm
Flexible fondant blade
Fine brush

1. Knead and soften the red rolled fondant. Roll a ball for Red's body. Place the ball into a toothpick set in Styrofoam. Allow the body to harden overnight.

2. Knead and soften the ivory rolled fondant. Roll very thin. Cut a circle using the 30 mm round cutter. Attach the ivory circle to the bird's belly using piping gel.

3. Knead and soften the white rolled fondant. Roll thin. Cut two circles using the 13 mm round cutter. Cut off the top fifth of each circle. Knead and soften the black rolled fondant. Roll two small black balls for the pupils. Attach the pupils to the white eyes using piping gel.

4. Roll the black fondant thin. Cut the eyebrows and the tail feathers using the flexible fondant blade.

5. Knead and soften the red rolled fondant. Roll two teardrops for the head feathers, making one a little larger than the other.

6. Knead and soften the orange rolled fondant. Form and cut the beak.

7. Add Red's features, using piping gel as the glue. First, attach the eyes and the eyebrows. Attach the beak. Finally, add the two red head feathers and the tail feathers. Using a fine brush, paint the ovals on the bird's cheeks using burgundy food coloring thinned slightly with water.

HAL

Green rolled fondant
White rolled fondant
Black rolled fondant
Orange rolled fondant
Piping gel
Round cutter, 13 mm
Round cutter, 30 mm
Flexible fondant blade

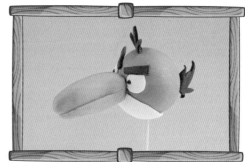

1. Knead and soften the green rolled fondant. Roll a ball for Hal's body. Place the ball into a toothpick set in Styrofoam. Allow the body to harden overnight.

2. Knead and soften the white rolled fondant. Roll very thin. Cut a circle using the 30 mm round cutter. Attach the white circle to the bird's belly using piping gel. Cut two white circles using the 13 mm round cutter. Cut off the top fifth of each circle.

3. Knead and soften the black rolled fondant. Roll two small black balls for the pupils. Attach the pupils to the white eyes using piping gel. Roll the black fondant thin. Cut the eyebrows, head feathers, and tail feathers using the flexible fondant blade.

4. Knead and soften the orange rolled fondant. Roll an elongated oval and form the beak. Use the flexible fondant blade to cut the beak.

5. Add Hal's features, using piping gel as the glue. First, attach the beak. Next, attach the eyes and the eyebrows. Finally, add the head and tail feathers.

BOMB

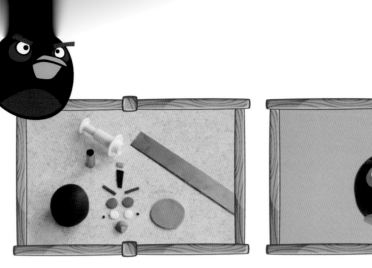

Black rolled fondant
Gray rolled fondant
White rolled fondant
Terra-cotta rolled fondant
Orange rolled fondant
Piping gel
Round cutter, 8 mm (white eyes)
Round cutter, 11 mm (gray eyes)
Round cutter, 30 mm
Flexible fondant blade

1. Knead and soften the black rolled fondant. Roll a ball for Bomb's body. Place the ball into a toothpick set in Styrofoam. Allow the body to harden overnight.

2. Knead and soften the gray rolled fondant. Roll very thin. Cut a circle using the 30 mm round cutter. Attach the gray circle to the bird's belly using piping gel. Cut two gray eye circles using the 11 mm round cutter. Cut off the top fifth of the eye at an angle for the eyebrow placement.

3. Knead and soften the white rolled fondant. Roll thin. Cut two inner eye circles using the 8 mm round cutter. Attach the inner eyes, off-center, to outer eyes using piping gel. Cut off the top fifth of the eye at an angle for the eyebrow placement.

4. Knead and soften the black rolled fondant. Roll two small black balls for the pupils. Attach the pupils to the white eyes using piping gel. Roll the black fondant thin. Cut the head feather using the flexible fondant blade.

5. Knead and soften the terra-cotta rolled fondant. Roll thin. Cut the eyebrows using the flexible fondant blade.

6. Knead and soften the orange rolled fondant. Form and cut the beak. Roll the orange fondant thin. Cut a small square for the top of his head feather. Attach it to the head feather with piping gel.

7. Add Bomb's features, using piping gel as the glue. First, attach the beak. Next, the eyes and the eyebrows. Finally, add the head feather.

CHUCK

Yellow rolled fondant
White rolled fondant
Black rolled fondant
Terra-cotta rolled fondant
Orange rolled fondant
Piping gel
Round cutter, 30 mm
Round cutter, 8 mm
Flexible fondant blade

1. Knead and soften the yellow rolled fondant. Roll a ball for Bomb's body. Then form the ball into triangle. Place the triangle into a toothpick set in Styrofoam. Allow the body to harden overnight.

2. Knead and soften the white rolled fondant. Roll very thin. Cut a circle using the 30 mm round cutter. Attach the white circle to the bird's belly using piping gel. Cut two white circles for eyes using the 8 mm round cutter. Cut off the top fifth of each eye.

3. Knead and soften the black rolled fondant. Roll two small black balls for the pupils. Attach the pupils to

the white eyes using piping gel. Roll the black fondant thin. Cut the black head feathers using the flexible fondant blade.

4. Knead and soften the terra-cotta rolled fondant. Roll thin. Cut the eyebrows using the flexible fondant blade.

5. Knead and soften the orange rolled fondant. Form and cut the beak.

6. Add Chuck's features, using piping gel as the glue. First, attach the beak. Next, attach the eyes and the eyebrows. Finally, add the black head feathers.

MATILDA

White rolled fondant
Ivory rolled fondant
Light green rolled fondant
Black rolled fondant
Orange rolled fondant
Piping gel
Round cutter, 8 mm
Round cutter, 11 mm
Round cutter, 30 mm
Oval cutter, 11 mm
Flexible fondant blade

1. Knead and soften the white rolled fondant. Roll a ball for Matilda's body. Then form the ball into an egg. Place the egg into a toothpick set in Styrofoam. Allow the body to harden overnight.

2. Knead and soften the ivory rolled fondant. Roll very thin. Cut a circle using the 30 mm round cutter. Attach the ivory circle to the bird's belly using piping gel.

3. Knead and soften the light green rolled fondant. Roll thin. Cut two ovals for the cheeks using the oval cutter.

4. Knead and soften the white rolled fondant. Roll thin. Cut two circles using the 11 mm round cutter. Cut off the bottom quarter of each circle using an 8 mm circle

cutter. Cut off the top fifth of the eye at an angle for the eyebrow placement.

5. Knead and soften the black rolled fondant. Roll two small black balls for the pupils. Attach the pupils to the white eyes using piping gel. Roll the black rolled fondant thin. Cut the black head feathers and the eyebrows using the flexible fondant blade.

6. Knead and soften the orange rolled fondant. Form and cut the beak.

7. Add Matilda's features, using piping gel as the glue. First, attach the beak. Next, attach the cheeks. Then the eyes and the eyebrows. Finally, add the black head feathers.

TERENCE

Red rolled fondant with
  a touch of brown added
Ivory rolled fondant
White rolled fondant
Black rolled fondant
Orange rolled fondant
Piping gel
Burgundy food coloring
Oval cutter, 48 mm x
  38 mm
Round cutter, 15 mm
Flexible fondant blade
Fine brush

1. Knead and soften the red rolled fondant. Roll a ball for Terence's body. Place the ball into a toothpick set in Styrofoam. Add wrinkles to Terence's forehead using the oval cutter. Allow the body to harden overnight.

2. Knead and soften the ivory rolled fondant. Roll very thin. Cut an oval using the 48 mm oval cutter. Cut notches on the sides of the ivory oval. Attach the ivory oval to the bird's belly using piping gel.

3. Knead and soften the white rolled fondant. Roll thin. Cut two eye circles using the 15 mm round cutter. Cut off the top third of each circle.

4. Knead and soften black rolled fondant. Roll two small black balls for the pupils. Attach the pupils to the white eyes using piping gel. Roll the black fondant thin. Cut the eyebrows using the flexible fondant blade.

5. Knead and soften the red rolled fondant. Roll two teardrops for head feathers, making one a little larger than the other.

6. Knead and soften the orange rolled fondant. Form and cut the beak.

7. Add Terence's features, using piping gel as the glue. First, attach the eyes and the eyebrows. Attach the beak. Finally, add the two red teardrops and the tail feathers. Using a fine brush, paint the ovals on the bird using burgundy food coloring thinned slightly with water.

Bad Piggies range in size and shape. Study the features before modeling the Bad Piggies. Note the position of the small, rounded ears. King Pig's two ears sit on one side of his head, while Forman Pig's ears sits on both sides of his head. One of Minion Pig's ears sits on one side of his head, while the other sits just off center on the other side. The position of the eyes is possibly the most important feature to make the Bad Piggies look authentic. The eyes are not above the nose, but are centered with the nose.

SHAPING THE BODIES

Before the Bad Piggies' bodies are made, insert toothpicks into Styrofoam. The toothpicks should extend out of the Styrofoam nearly the height, but not any taller, than the Bad Piggies that will be made. All of the Bad Piggies' bodies start with a round shape. The Minion Pigs and King Pig are round with a slight tapered top. Foreman Pig is round and tapered more than the Minion Pigs and King Pig. Corporal Pig is round, but tapers slightly at the bottom. Form the bodies and place them on the toothpick. Use the chart on page 26 and 27 for guidelines when sizing the bodies.

SHAPING THE NOSES

To shape the nose, form a ball and flatten it into an oval shape. Use a ball tool to indent the nostrils. The Minion Pigs and Corporal Pig have one round nostril and one oval nostril. Foreman Pig has kidney-shaped nostrils. King Pig has teardrop-shaped nostrils.

The nostrils can be painted with dark green food coloring that is slightly thinned with water instead of filling in the nostrils with dark green fondant.

Roll dark green rolled fondant into small balls or ovals and insert them into the indented nostrils, using piping gel to attach.

FORMING THE EARS

To shape the ears, form a ball. Use a ball tool to indent the ears. Cut the bottom fifth of the ball to level one edge.

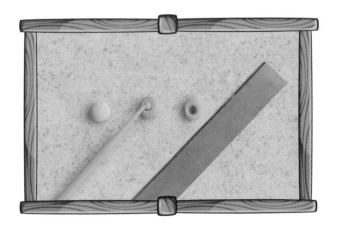

SHAPING THE EYEBROWS

All of the Bad Piggies except for Foreman Pig have small, skinny, dark green eyebrows. Knead and soften dark green rolled fondant (or orange fondant for Foreman Pig). Pinch a small piece and roll into a short snake.

MINION PIGS

Green rolled fondant
Light green rolled fondant
Dark green rolled fondant
White rolled fondant
Piping gel
Black nonpareils
Round cutter, 15 mm
Ball modeling tool
Flexible fondant blade

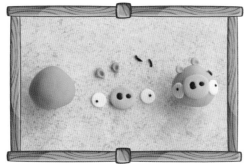 

1. Knead and soften green rolled fondant. Roll a ball for Minion Pig's body. Slightly taper at the top of the ball. Place the ball into a toothpick set in Styrofoam. Allow the body to harden overnight.

2. Knead and soften green fondant. Roll two balls for the ears. Emboss two holes in the ears using the ball modeling tool. Cut the bottom of the ears using the flexible fondant blade.

3. Knead and soften light green rolled fondant. Form a ball. Flatten to form an oval for the snout. Emboss the nostrils with the ball modeling tool. Knead and soften dark green rolled fondant. Form two small balls sized to fit inside the nostrils. Attach the nostrils to the nose with piping gel. Roll two small, thin snakes for the eyebrows.

4. Knead and soften white rolled fondant. Roll thin. Cut two eye circles using the 15 mm round cutter. Attach black nonpareils (for the pupils) to the white eyes using piping gel.

5. Add the Pig's features, using piping gel as the glue. First, attach the nose and the ears. Next, attach the eyes and the eyebrows.

CORPORAL PIG

Green rolled fondant
Light green rolled fondant
Dark green rolled fondant
White rolled fondant
Brown rolled fondant
Gray rolled fondant
Light gray rolled fondant
Piping gel
Black nonpareils
Ball modeling tool
Round cutter, 13 mm
Round cutter, 45 mm
Oval cutter, 10 mm x 8 mm
Oval cutter, 13 mm x 11 mm
Flexible fondant blade

1. Knead and soften green rolled fondant. Roll a ball for Corporal Pig's body. Slightly taper at the center of the ball. Place the ball into a toothpick set in Styrofoam. Allow the body to harden overnight.

2. Knead and soften light green rolled fondant. Form a ball. Flatten to form an oval for the snout. Emboss the nostrils with a small ball modeling tool. Knead and soften dark

(continued)

green rolled fondant. Form two small balls sized to fit inside the nostrils. Attach the nostrils to the nose with piping gel. Roll two small, thin snakes for the eyebrows.

3. Knead and soften white rolled fondant. Roll thin. Cut two eye circles using the 13 mm round cutter. Cut an oval for the helmet reflection using the 10 mm x 8 mm cutter. Attach black nonpareils (for the pupils) to the white eyes using piping gel.

4. Knead and soften brown rolled fondant. Cut two small strips for the helmet straps. Emboss small holes in the straps using a toothpick.

5. Knead and soften gray rolled fondant. Cut a circle for the helmet using the 45 mm cutter. Cut a small pie shape out of the circle using a fondant blade. Form the helmet on the pig using piping gel to attach. Cut a small, gray square for the helmet strap.

6. Knead and soften light gray rolled fondant. Cut an oval for the underlayer of the helmet reflection using the 13 mm x 11 mm cutter.

7. Add the pig's features, using piping gel as the glue. First, attach the nose and eyes. Next, attach the helmet straps, eyebrows, and helmet reflection.

FOREMAN PIG

Green rolled fondant
Light green rolled fondant
Dark green rolled fondant
Orange rolled fondant
White rolled fondant
Piping gel
Black nonpareils
Round cutter, 15 mm
Ball modeling tool
Flexible fondant blade

1. Knead and soften green rolled fondant. Roll a ball for Foreman Pig's body. Slightly taper at the top of the ball. Place the ball into a toothpick set in Styrofoam. Allow the body to harden overnight.

2. Knead and soften green fondant. Roll two balls for the ears. Emboss two holes in the ears using the small ball modeling tool. Cut the bottom of the ears using the flexible fondant blade.

3. Knead and soften light green rolled fondant. Form a ball. Flatten to form an oval for the snout. Emboss the nostrils with a small ball modeling tool. Knead and soften dark green rolled fondant. Form two small ovals sized to fit inside the nostrils. Attach the nostrils to the nose with piping gel.

4. Knead and soften orange rolled fondant. Roll two small, thin snakes for the eyebrows.

5. Roll orange fondant thin. Cut the moustache using a flexible fondant blade.

6. Knead and soften white rolled fondant. Roll thin. Cut two eye circles using the 15 mm round cutter. Attach black nonpareils (for the pupils) to the white eyes using piping gel.

7. Add the pig's features, using piping gel as the glue. First, attach the moustache and the ears. Next, attach the nose, eyes, and eyebrows.

KING PIG

Green rolled fondant
Light green rolled fondant
Dark green rolled fondant
Yellow rolled fondant
Blue rolled fondant
White rolled fondant
Black rolled fondant
Piping gel
Round cutter, 19 mm
Ball modeling tool
Flexible fondant blade

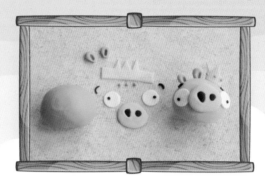

1. Knead and soften green rolled fondant. Roll a ball for King Pig's body. Slightly taper at the top of the ball. Place the ball into a toothpick set in Styrofoam. Allow the body to harden overnight.

2. Knead and soften green fondant. Roll two balls for the ears. Emboss two holes in the ears using the small ball modeling tool. Cut the bottom of the ears using the flexible fondant blade.

3. Knead and soften light green rolled fondant. Form a ball. Flatten to form an oval for the snout. Emboss the nostrils with a small ball modeling tool. Knead and soften dark green rolled fondant. Roll two small snakes for the eyebrows. Form two small ovals sized to fit inside the nostrils. Attach the nostrils to the nose with piping gel.

4. Knead and soften yellow rolled fondant. Cut the crown using a flexible fondant blade. Arrange the crown on the head. Knead and soften blue rolled fondant. Roll three small balls for the crown accents.

5. Knead and soften white rolled fondant. Roll thin. Cut two eye circles using the 19 mm round cutter. Knead and soften black rolled fondant. Roll two small balls for the pupils. Attach the pupils to the white eyes using piping gel.

6. Add the pig's features, using piping gel as the glue. First, attach the nose and the eyes. Next, add the eyebrows, ears, and crown accents.

DAMAGED BAD PIGGIES

Green rolled fondant
Light green rolled fondant
Dark green rolled fondant
White rolled fondant
Purple rolled fondant
Red rolled fondant
Piping gel
Black nonpareils
Round cutter, 15 mm
Ball modeling tool
Flexible fondant blade

1. Knead and soften green rolled fondant. Roll a ball for Damaged Pig's body. Slightly taper at the top of the ball. Place the ball into a toothpick set in Styrofoam. Add a small flattened half circle to the side of the head for a knot. Allow the body to harden overnight.

2. Knead and soften green fondant. Roll two balls for the ears. Emboss two holes in the ears using the small ball modeling tool. Cut the bottom of the ears using the flexible fondant blade.

3. Knead and soften light green rolled fondant. Form a ball. Flatten to form an oval for the snout. Emboss the nostrils with a small ball modeling tool. Knead and soften dark green rolled fondant. Form two small balls sized to fit inside the nostrils. Attach the nostrils to the nose with piping gel. Roll two small, thin snakes for the eyebrows. Flatten an oval for the mouth.

4. Knead and soften white rolled fondant. Form three small ovals for the teeth. Roll white fondant thin. Cut two circles for the eyes using the 15 mm round cutter. Attach black nonpareils (for the pupils) to the white eyes using piping gel.

5. Knead and soften purple rolled fondant. Roll thin. Cut two circles using the 15 mm round cutter. Cut the circles in half to make eyelids.

6. Knead and soften red rolled fondant. Form a teardrop for the tongue. Flatten the teardrop and emboss a line using a toothpick.

7. Add the pig's features, using piping gel as the glue. First, attach the mouth. Next attach the nose, teeth, and ears. Next, attach the eyes, eyelids, tongue, and eyebrows.

SCARED BAD PIGGIES

Green rolled fondant
Light green rolled fondant
Dark green rolled fondant
White rolled fondant
Piping gel
Black nonpareils
Round cutter, 15 mm
Ball modeling tool
Flexible fondant blade

1. Knead and soften green rolled fondant. Roll a ball for Scared Pig's body. Slightly taper at the top of the ball. Place the ball into a toothpick set in Styrofoam. Allow the body to harden overnight.

2. Knead and soften green fondant. Roll two balls for the ears. Emboss two holes in the ears using the small ball modeling tool. Cut the bottom of the ears using the flexible fondant blade.

3. Knead and soften light green rolled fondant. Form a ball. Flatten to form an oval for the snout. Emboss the nostrils with a small ball modeling tool. Knead and soften dark green rolled fondant. Form two small balls sized to fit inside the nostrils. Attach the nostrils to the nose with piping gel. Roll two small, thin snakes for the eyebrows. Flatten an oval for the mouth.

4. Knead and soften white rolled fondant. Form five small ovals for the teeth. Roll white fondant thin. Cut two circles for the eyes using the 15 mm round cutter. Attach black nonpareils (for the pupils) to the white eyes using piping gel.

5. Add the pig's features, using piping gel as the glue. First, attach the mouth. Next attach the nose, teeth, and ears. Finally, attach the eyes and eyebrows.

The structures are simply different lengths of rectangles. The rectangles shown are in dark ivory, but they can be made in gray as well. It imperative to make these structures ahead of time to ensure they are strong. Toothpicks are used to build the structures. Do not cut the toothpicks, or the toothpicks may become a choking hazard.

BLOCKS

Dark ivory or gray rolled
    fondant
Piping gel
Flexible fondant blade
Toothpicks

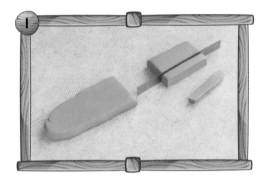 

1. Knead and soften ivory rolled fondant. Roll the fondant approximately 12 mm thick. Cut straight down into the fondant to create rectangles.

2. Continue cutting several rectangles. Insert toothpicks in the ends of rectangles that will be inserted into the cake. Insert toothpicks into the other end of the rectangles that will be used to build the upper part of the structure.

3. Secure the pieces together with the toothpicks and piping gel. Continue adding toothpicks and more rectangles to build the desired structure. Allow the pieces to harden for several days before placing them on the cake.

CATAPULT

Dark ivory rolled fondant
Brown rolled fondant
Piping gel
Flexible fondant blade
Toothpicks

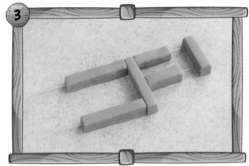 

1. Knead and soften dark ivory rolled fondant. Form a misshapen triangle. Cut straight down into the fondant and cut a triangle from the center. Round the edges to soften. Insert a toothpick halfway into the bottom of the catapult.

2. Knead and soften brown rolled fondant. Roll thin. Using a fondant blade, cut one long strip and two short strips of fondant. Attach the long strip to each side of the catapult using piping gel. Use the two shorter strips to hide the seam.

Cakes

The cakes in this section are filled with colorful and fun Angry Birds and Minion Pigs. Copy the cakes as they are, or use the cakes for inspiration to create your own Angry Birds design. The first few cakes are great for beginners or if you are short on time. The later cakes have lots of details that appeal to children and adults. These cakes will require extra time. Most of the decorations for these cakes can be made ahead. Some of the decorations require you to make them ahead for stability. The amount of fondant needed to create the accents will depend on the thickness rolled; however, the amount needed is typically less than an ounce (28 g) per color. The amount of fondant needed to cover the cake will also vary depending on the thickness rolled. See page 23 for a helpful chart.

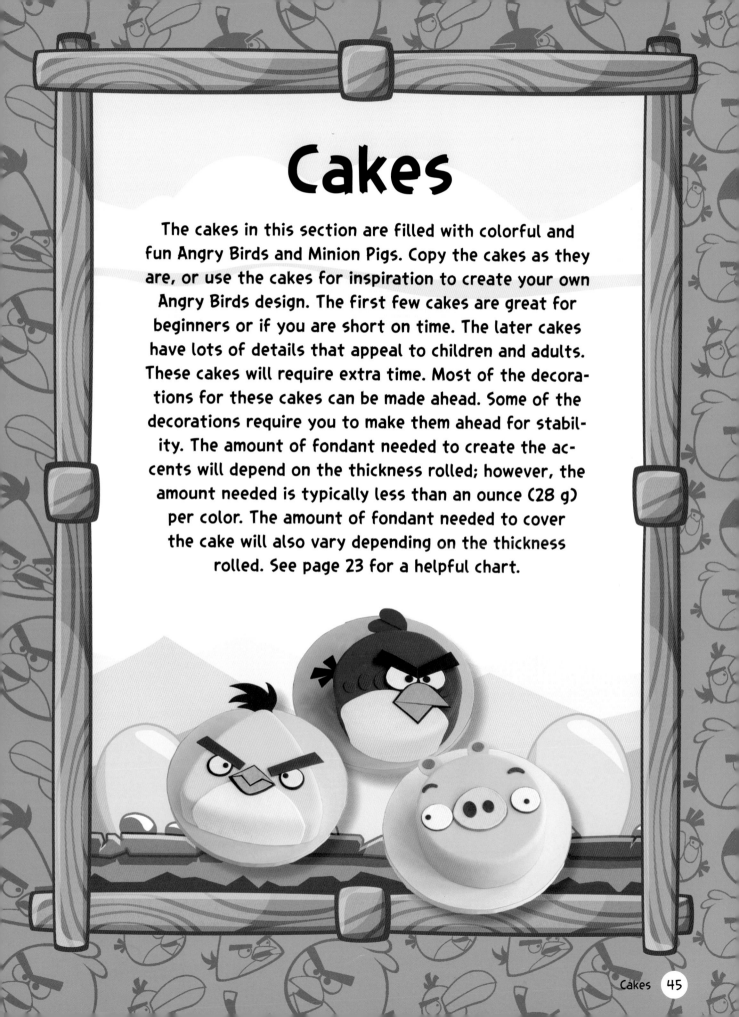

Cakes with Appliqué Details

The following cakes have accents made of rolled fondant that are pieced together for an appliqué style. Patterns are included on pages 88 to 90 for the appliqué details. Either rolled fondant or gum paste can be used for the face details, but it is important to use gum paste, and not rolled fondant, for any accents that will extend from the cake. The Bad Piggies' ears, Chuck's head feathers, and Red's tail and head feathers should be made several days ahead to allow ample time for the pieces to harden. Gum paste accents that are made in humid climates will likely take longer to dry and may possibly begin to distort once placed on the cake. If the cake will be made in an area with high humidity, insert the pieces that extend from the cake just before displaying the cake.

MAKING THE APPLIQUÉ DETAILS

Roll gum paste thin. Trace and cut the pattern for the desired cake on pages 88 to 90. Place the cut pattern on top of the rolled gum paste. Trim around using a mini pizza cutter or polymer clay blade.

A mini pizza cutter is best for cutting straight lines and for rounded corners.

A clay blade is the best to cut straight lines or to cut into sharp, angled corners.

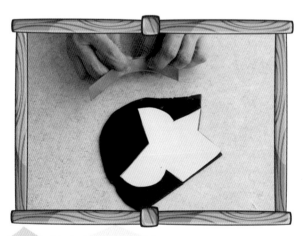

A clay blade is also ideal for cutting curves because it is thin and flexible to shape.

Round cutters are used for the eyes on the Minion Pig and Chuck.

Cakes with Appliqué Details

MAKING THE CONTRASTING COLOR FOR THE BIRDS' BELLY

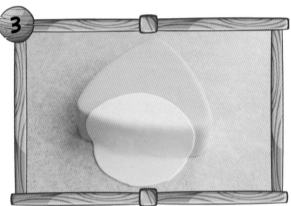

1. Roll rolled fondant to 2 mm. Place a clean, 8" (20.3 cm) round pan on top of the rolled fondant. Trim around the pan to create an 8" (20.3 cm) circle.

2. Turn the circle over and brush on piping gel.

3. Place the circle on the fondant-covered cake. Trim around the bottom to remove excess.

INSERTING ACCENTS THAT EXTEND PAST THE CAKE

1. Accents such as the head feather on the yellow bird, ears on the pig, and tail feathers on the red bird should be made in gum paste. Allow the gum paste accent to harden for several days. For ease in inserting the piece, puncture the fondant-covered cake with a knife, creating a slit where the accent will be inserted. Gently insert the accent.

Tip!

- These cakes are perfect for those who prefer buttercream icing rather than rolled fondant. Accents should still be made in rolled fondant and gum paste, but the cake can be iced in buttercream.
- Not much time for baking and decorating before the party? Cover the board with rolled fondant and make the accents for these cakes up to several weeks ahead of time. Then, all that is needed on the baking and decorating day is baking the cake, covering the cake with rolled fondant, and then arranging the details on the birds or pigs.
- The approximate serving size is listed for each cake. These cakes are easy to duplicate in other sizes if fewer or more servings are needed. Enlarge or decrease the pattern as desired.

RED

Serves 24

Blue rolled fondant
White rolled fondant
Orange rolled fondant
Burgundy rolled fondant
Red rolled fondant
Ivory rolled fondant
Buttercream frosting
Piping gel
Black gum paste
Red gum paste
Mini pizza cutter

Round cutter, 13 mm
Round cutter, 15 mm
Oval cutter, 26 mm x 22 mm
Oval cutter, 35 mm x 25 mm
Oval cutter, 48 mm x 38 mm
Flexible fondant blade
14" (35.6 cm) base board
9" (23 cm) round cake pan
8" (20.3 cm) round cake pan
9" (23 cm) plastic board or
    greaseproof cardboard

1. Cover the base board with blue rolled fondant. Trace and cut apart the pattern for Red on page 88. The tail and head feather accents should be made several days ahead of time. The face accents can be made several days ahead of time if desired, but it is not necessary.

2. Roll black gum paste thin. Cut the tail feather using the fondant blade. Cut the eyebrows using the fondant blade. Cut the face outline using the fondant blade. Cut the pupils of the eye using a 13 mm cutter for one eye and the 15 mm cutter for the other.

3. Roll red gum paste thin. Cut the head feathers using the fondant blade.

4. Roll white rolled fondant thin. Cut the eyes using the fondant blade.

5. Roll orange rolled fondant thin. Cut the two beak parts using the fondant blade or a mini pizza cutter.

6. Roll burgundy rolled fondant thin. Cut the oval face accents using the three oval cutters. Cut one of the small ovals, one of the medium oval, and two of the large ovals. Trim the ends of the larger oval.

7. Bake and cool two single layer 9" (23 cm) cakes. Sandwich the two single layer cakes using buttercream. Place the cake on a 9" (23 cm) cardboard. Ice the cake in buttercream. Cover the cake with red rolled fondant. Roll ivory fondant to 2 mm. Use the clean, 8" (20.3 cm) cake pan as a pattern to create a large circle for the belly. Brush piping gel on the back of the cut circle. Place the circle on the cake. Transfer the 9" (23 cm) cake to the 14" (35.6 cm) covered base board, placing the bird toward the bottom of the board to allow room for the head feathers.

8. Place the face detail on the cake. The face outline and eyebrows will not lie flat because of the extra 2 mm height made from the belly. Place 2 mm rolled pieces of red fondant scraps underneath the face outline and the eyebrows for the accents to lie flat. Arrange the eyebrows, eyes, pupils, beak, and oval face details on the cake, using piping gel to attach.

9. Insert the head feathers and tail feathers just before displaying the cake.

CHUCK

Serves 20

Blue rolled fondant
White rolled fondant
Orange rolled fondant
Terra-cotta rolled fondant
Yellow rolled fondant
Black gum paste
Piping gel
Buttercream frosting
Round cutter, 45 mm

Round cutter, 8 mm
Round cutter, 40 mm
Flexible fondant blade
14" (35.6 cm) base board
10" (24.5 cm) convex triangle cake pan
8" (20.3 cm) round cake pan
10" (24.5 cm) triangle greaseproof cardboard

1. Cover the base board with blue rolled fondant. Trace and cut apart the pattern for Chuck on page 89. The head feather accent should be made several days ahead of time. The face accents can be made several days ahead of time if desired, but it is not necessary.

2. Roll black gum paste thin. Cut the head feather using the fondant blade. Cut the beak outline using the fondant blade. Cut the eye using the 45 mm round cutter. Cut the pupils of the eyes using the 8 mm cutter.

3. Roll white rolled fondant thin. Cut the eyes using the 40 mm cutter. Layer the white and black of the eyes, using piping gel to glue together. Use the fondant blade to cut off the top one-fifth of the eyes.

4. Roll orange rolled fondant thin. Cut the two beak parts using the fondant blade.

5. Roll terra-cotta rolled fondant thin. Cut the eyebrows.

6. Bake and cool two single layer 10" (25.4 cm) triangle cakes. Sandwich the two single layer cakes using buttercream. Cut a greaseproof cardboard triangle exactly the size of the triangle cake, using the pan as a pattern to cut around. Place the cake on the cut cardboard. Ice the cake in buttercream. Cover the cake with yellow rolled fondant.

7. Roll white fondant to 2 mm. Use the clean, 8" (20.3 cm) cake pan as a pattern to create a large circle for the belly. Brush piping gel on the back of the cut circle. Place the circle on the cake. Trim around the bottom of the circle. Transfer the cake to the 14" (35.6 cm) covered base board.

8. Place the face detail on the cake. The beak background will not lie flat because of the extra 2 mm height made from the belly. Place 2 mm rolled pieces of yellow fondant scraps underneath the beak background for it to lie flat.

9. Arrange the eyes, eyebrows, pupils, and beak on the cake, using piping gel to attach. Insert the head feathers just before displaying the cake.

BAD PIGGIE

Serves 24

Blue rolled fondant
Dark green rolled fondant
Medium dark green rolled fondant
Light green rolled fondant
White rolled fondant
Black rolled fondant
Green rolled fondant
Green gum paste
Piping gel
Buttercream frosting
Round cutter, 22 mm
Round cutter, 56 mm
Round cutter, 48 mm
Round cutter, 8 mm
Oval cutter, 26 mm x 22 mm
Oval cutter, 35 mm x 25 mm
Flexible fondant blade
14" (35.6 cm) base board
9" (23 cm) round cake pan
9" (23 cm) plastic board or greaseproof cardboard

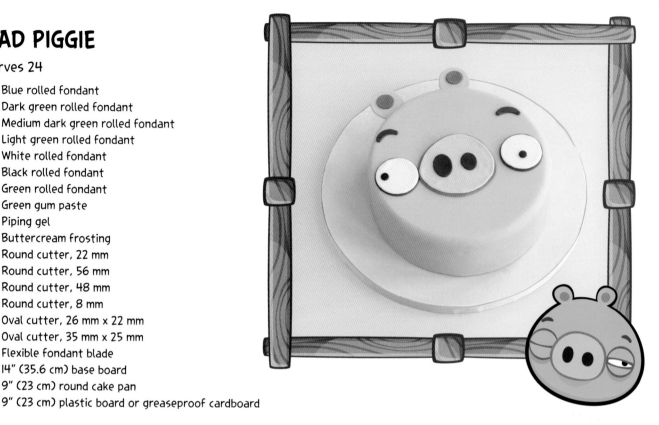

1. Cover the base board with blue rolled fondant. Trace and cut apart the patterns for the ear, pig nose, and nose outline on page 90. The ears should be made several days ahead of time. The face accents can be made several days ahead of time if desired, but it is not necessary.

2. Roll green gum paste thin. Cut the ears using the fondant blade.

3. Roll medium dark green fondant thin. Cut two circles for the ear details using the 22 mm round cutter. Cut the larger nose piece.

4. Roll light green rolled fondant thin. Cut the smaller nose piece.

5. Roll dark green rolled fondant thin. Cut the eye outlines using the 56 mm round cutter. Cut two eyebrows using the fondant blade.

6. Roll white rolled fondant thin. Cut the eyes using the 48 mm round cutter.

7. Roll black rolled fondant thin. Cut the pupils of the eyes using the 8 mm cutter. Cut the nostrils using the oval cutters.

8. Bake and cool two single layer 9" (23 cm) cakes. Sandwich the two single layer cakes using buttercream. Place the cake on a 9" (23 cm) cardboard. Ice the cake in buttercream. Cover the cake with green rolled fondant. Transfer the 9" (23 cm) cake to the 14" (35.6 cm) covered base board.

9. Place the face detail on the cake. Arrange the eyes, nose, nostrils, and eyebrows on the cake, using piping gel to attach.

10. Insert the ears just before displaying the cake.

Sheet Cake Variations

The face details and colors of Angry Birds and Bad Piggies are very recognizable. For the easiest decorated cake, simply cut the face decorations and place on a rolled fondant-covered or butter-cream-iced sheet cake. Bad Piggies and Red are the two sheet cakes shown; however, choose any of the bird or pig faces for these sheet cakes using the patterns on pages 88 to 91. There's no need for pieces such as ears or head feathers, which extend past the cake, because face details are the only thing needed to make your sheet cake recognizable.

RED

Serves 20

Black rolled fondant
White rolled fondant
Orange rolled fondant
Red rolled fondant
Buttercream frosting
Piping gel
Round cutter, 13 mm
Round cutter, 15 mm
Mini pizza cutter
Flexible fondant blade
10" x 14" (25.4 x 35.6 cm) base board
9" x 13" (23 x 33 cm) quarter sheet
   cake pan

1. Enlarge the pattern for Red on page 88 to 120 percent. Cut apart the pattern. Knead and soften black rolled fondant. Roll thin. Cut the eyebrows using the fondant blade. Cut the face outline using the fondant blade. Cut the pupils of the eye using a 13 mm cutter for one eye and the 15 mm cutter for the other.

2. Roll white rolled fondant thin. Cut the eyes using the fondant blade.

3. Roll orange rolled fondant thin. Cut the two beak parts using the fondant blade or a mini pizza cutter.

4. Place the face outline on the cake. Arrange the eyebrows, eyes, pupils, and beak on the cake, using piping gel to attach.

BAD PIGGIES

Serves 20

Medium green rolled fondant
Light green rolled fondant
Dark green rolled fondant
White rolled fondant
Black rolled fondant
Purple rolled fondant
Light purple rolled fondant
Red rolled fondant
Light red rolled fondant
Green rolled fondant
Piping gel
Buttercream frosting

Round cutter, 56 mm
Round cutter, 48 mm
Round cutter, 8 mm
Round cutter, 65 mm
Oval cutter, 26 mm x 22 mm
Oval cutter, 35 mm x 25 mm
Oval cutter, 80 mm x 62 mm
Flexible fondant blade
10" x 14" (25.4 x 35.6 cm)
    base board
9" x 13" (23 x 33 cm) quarter
    sheet cake pan

1. Trace and cut apart the patterns for the pig nose, nose outline, tongue, and tongue outline on page 90. Roll medium green rolled fondant thin. Cut the nose outline using the fondant blade. Roll light green rolled fondant thin. Cut the nose using the fondant blade. Layer the two nose pieces using piping gel to adhere. Roll dark green rolled fondant thin. Cut one nostrils using the 26 mm x 22 mm oval cutter and the other nostril using the 35 mm x 25 mm oval cutter. Cut two eyebrows using the fondant blade. Cut the mouth using the 80 mm x 62 mm oval cutter. Cut two circles for the eye outlines using the 56 mm round cutter. Cut three ovals for the teeth outlines using the 35 mm x 25 mm oval cutter.

2. Roll white rolled fondant thin. Cut the eyes using the 48 mm round cutter. Cut three teeth using the 26 mm x 22 mm oval cutter. Layer each of the small white ovals on the 35 mm x 25 mm ovals using piping gel to adhere. Cut the layered ovals in half for the teeth. Layer the eyes using piping gel to adhere.

3. Roll black rolled fondant thin. Cut the pupils of the eyes using the 8 mm cutter. Place the pupils on the eyes using piping gel to adhere.

4. Roll purple rolled fondant thin. Cut the eyelid outlines using the 65 mm round cutter. Cut the circles in half. Roll light purple rolled fondant thin. Cut the eyelids using the 56 mm round cutter. Cut the circles in half. Layer the eyelid and eyelid outline using piping gel to adhere.

5. Roll red rolled fondant thin. Cut the tongue outline using the pattern and the fondant blade. Roll light red rolled fondant thin. Cut the tongue using the pattern and the fondant blade. Layer the tongue. Emboss the tongue using a toothpick.

6. Place the face detail on the cake using piping gel to attach. Arrange the mouth, nose, teeth, and tongue. Next add the eyes and eyelids. Finally add the eyebrows.

Tiered Cake with Appliqué Details

This three-tier cake is an impressive but easy cake to decorate and it serves more than 50 people. Follow the instructions for appliqué style cutting on page 47 to cut the features of the Angry Birds.

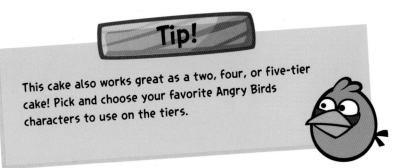

Tip!

This cake also works great as a two, four, or five-tier cake! Pick and choose your favorite Angry Birds characters to use on the tiers.

Serves 50

Blue rolled fondant	Flexible fondant blade
Black rolled fondant	14" (45.7 cm) base board
White rolled fondant	Two 6" (15.2 cm) round cake pans
Orange rolled fondant	Two 8" (20.3 cm) round cake pans
Terra-cotta rolled fondant	Two 10" (25.4 cm) round cake pans
Red rolled fondant	6" (15.2 cm) plastic board or grease-proof cardboard
Burgundy rolled fondant	8" (20.3 cm) plastic board or grease-proof cardboard
Yellow rolled fondant	10" (25.4 cm) plastic board or grease-proof cardboard
Sky blue rolled fondant	Ribbon
Piping gel	Hot glue gun
Buttercream frosting	Dowel rods
Mini pizza cutter	
Round cutter, 12 mm	
Round cutter, 13 mm	
Round cutter, 15 mm	
Round cutter, 40 mm	
Round cutter, 48 mm	
Oval cutter, 35 mm x 25 mm	

BASE BOARD AND CAKE PREPARATION

1. Cover the base board with sky blue rolled fondant. Attach a ribbon around the edge of the board with a hot glue gun. Set aside.

2. Bake and cool two single layer cakes in each of the sizes listed. For each layer, sandwich the two single layer cakes using buttercream. Place the two-layer cake on a cake board of the same size. Ice the cake in buttercream. Cover the cake with the appropriate color of rolled fondant.

BLUE BIRD TIER

1. Trace and cut apart the pattern for the blue bird on page 91. Roll black fondant to 2 mm. Cut the face outline using the fondant blade. Attach the

black face outline to the blue fondant-covered cake using piping gel. Cut the pupils of the eye using a 12 mm cutter.

2. Roll white rolled fondant thin. Cut the eyes using the fondant blade.

3. Roll orange rolled fondant thin. Cut the two beak parts using the fondant blade or a mini pizza cutter.

4. Roll terra-cotta rolled fondant thin. Cut the cheek accents using the fondant blade.

5. Add the features to the face using piping gel to adhere.

RED TIER

1. Trace and cut apart the pattern for front-facing Red on page 91. Roll black fondant to 2 mm. Cut the eyebrows using the fondant blade. Cut the face outline using the fondant blade. Attach the black face outline to the red fondant-covered cake using piping gel. Cut the pupils of the eye using a 13 mm cutter.

2. Roll white rolled fondant thin. Cut the eyes using the fondant blade.

3. Roll orange rolled fondant thin. Cut the two beak parts using the fondant blade or a mini pizza cutter.

4. Roll burgundy rolled fondant thin. Cut the ovals using the 35 mm x 25 mm oval cutter. Trim the ovals to fit beside the black face outline.

5. Add the features to the face using piping gel to adhere.

CHUCK TIER

1. Reduce the pattern on page 89 for Chuck by 70 percent. Cut apart the patterns for the beak, beak outline, and eyebrows. Roll black fondant to 2 mm. Cut the beak outline using the fondant blade. Cut the eye outline using the 48 mm round cutter. Cut the pupils of the eyes using the 15 mm cutter.

2. Roll white rolled fondant thin. Cut the eyes using the 40 mm cutter. Layer the white and black of the eyes, using piping gel to glue together. Use the fondant blade to cut off the top one-fifth of the eyes.

3. Roll orange rolled fondant thin. Cut the two beak parts using the fondant blade.

4. Roll terra-cotta rolled fondant thin. Cut the eyebrows.

5. Attach the black beak outline to the yellow fondant-covered cake using piping gel. Add the rest of the features to the face using piping gel to adhere.

ASSEMBLING

Stack the cake following the instructions on page 22, using dowels between each layer. Be sure to use icing between to serve as a glue for the tiers.

Square Mod Angry Birds Cake

Serves 56

Green rolled fondant
Light blue rolled fondant
Yellow rolled fondant
Red rolled fondant
Ivory rolled fondant
Black rolled fondant
White rolled fondant
Orange rolled fondant
Burgundy rolled fondant
Blue rolled fondant
Piping gel
Buttercream frosting
Mini pizza cutter
Round cutter, 4 ½" (11.4 cm)
Round cutter, 8 mm
Oval cutter, 10 mm x 13 mm
Oval cutter, 13 mm x 17 mm
Oval cutter, 22 mm x 16 mm
Paisley cutter
Flexible fondant blade
Pen fine blade utility knife
14" (35.6 cm) square base board
Two 8" (20.3 cm) square pans
Two 10" (25.4 cm) square pans
8" (20.3 cm) square plastic board or greaseproof cardboard
10" (25.4 cm) square plastic board or greaseproof cardboard
Ribbon
Hot glue gun
Dowels
Ruler

This two-tier cake has a modern design, with a single Angry Bird featured. To save time, Red and all of the dots can be made ahead of time. The head feathers on Red should be made ahead of time so they are firm when placed on the stripes.

1. Cover the base board with green rolled fondant. Attach a ribbon with hot glue around the edge of the board. Set aside.

2. Bake and cool two single layer cakes in each of the sizes listed. For each layer, sandwich the two single layer cakes using buttercream. Place the two-layer cake on a cake board of the same size. Ice the cake in buttercream. Cover the cake with the appropriate color of rolled fondant. Place the 10" (25.4 cm) cake on the fondant-covered board. Stack the cake following the instructions on page 22.

3. Trace and cut the pattern for the blue stripes on page 92. Knead and soften blue rolled fondant. Roll thin. Place the stripe pattern on the rolled fondant. Cut around the pattern using a pizza cutter.

4. Brush piping gel on the back of the stripe. Place the stripe on the cake with the widest end at the bottom. Repeat, adding seven more stripes in the pattern shown. Center a round 4 1/2" (11.4 cm) cutter on the top of the cake. Gently press so the cutter cuts through the stripes, but not the cake.

5. Lift the cutter and remove the excess center pieces, leaving a clean circle in the center of the cake.

6. Knead and soften red rolled fondant. Roll to 4 mm thick. Cut a circle using the 4 1/2" (11.4 cm) round cutter. Use the same cutter and cut off the bottom one-fourth of the circle. Repeat with ivory rolled fondant. Replace the red cut piece with the ivory cut piece. Arrange the face on the cut circle on top tier, fitting it into the circle.

7. Reduce the pattern on page 91 by 80 percent for front-facing Red. Cut apart the pattern. Roll black fondant to 2 mm. Cut the eyebrows using the fondant blade. Cut the face outline using the fine utility knife. Cut the pupils of the eye using the 8 mm cutter. Roll white rolled fondant thin. Cut the eyes using the utility knife. Roll orange rolled fondant thin. Cut the two beak parts using the fondant blade. Roll burgundy rolled fondant thin. Cut the ovals using the three cutters. Attach the black face outline to the red circle on the cake using piping gel to adhere. Add the features to the face using piping gel to adhere.

8. Roll red fondant to 2 mm. Cut two head feathers using a paisley cutter.

9. Arrange the head feathers on Red.

10. Cut red, black, orange, green, and blue rolled fondant circles using the 15 mm round cutter. Attach to the lower tier using piping gel. Use a ruler to keep the dots straight and to evenly space the dots.

Sheet Cake with Angry Birds Scene

Capture the excitement of the game by molding a slingshot with Red about to launch and destroy! Red is used for the bird, but any of the birds can be used in his place. The slingshot (except the band) and structures must be made several days ahead to allow ample time for the pieces to harden. Toothpicks are used to assemble the structure for the pigs. Never cut the toothpicks, as a short toothpick is a choking hazard.

1. Cover the cake board with dark blue rolled fondant.

2. Mold a slingshot following the instructions on page 44. Form the slingshot on a can. Insert a toothpick halfway into the bottom of the slingshot base. Allow the slingshot to harden for several days.

Serves 20

- Dark blue rolled fondant
- Green rolled fondant
- Medium green rolled fondant
- Light green rolled fondant
- Dark green rolled fondant
- Brown rolled fondant
- Hand-modeled slingshot
- Hand-modeled structure pieces
- Hand-modeled bird of choice
- Hand-modeled pigs
- Buttercream frosting
- Piping gel
- Flexible fondant blade
- 10" x 14" (25.4 x 35.6 cm) cake board
- 9" x 13" (23 x 33 cm) quarter sheet cake pan
- Toothpick

3. Build the structures as on page 44. Allow the structures to harden for several days.

4. Bake and cool a single layer 9" x 13" (23 x 33 cm) sheet cake. Ice the cake in buttercream. Cover the cake with green rolled fondant.

5. Knead and soften medium green rolled fondant. Roll the fondant into a ball and flatten. Cut with a fondant blade to create grass. Shape the grass to create movement. Repeat, creating tufts of grass in light green and dark green.

6. Roll brown rolled fondant thin. Cut a strip of fondant for the band of the slingshot. Cut two small strips.

7. Insert the slingshot into the cake. Place the bird on the cake and wrap the band around the bird. Attach the band to the slingshot with piping gel. Add the two smaller pieces to hide the seam. Place tufts of grass here and there on the cake.

8. Arrange the structures, Bad Piggies, and additional grass on the cake.

Round Cake with Angry Birds Scene

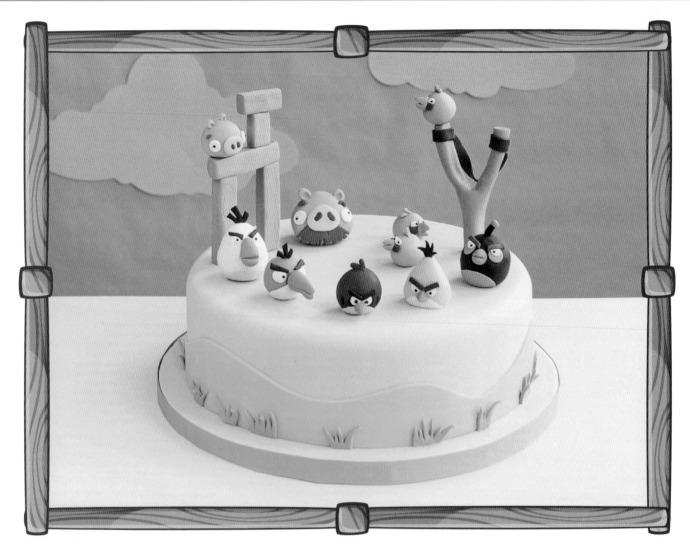

Those thieving pigs won't get away with stealing all the Angry Birds' eggs! Nearly all the popular characters are represented on this cake. The slingshot (except the band) and structures must be made several days ahead to allow ample time for the pieces to harden. Toothpicks are used to assemble the structure for the pigs. Never cut the toothpicks, as a short toothpick is a choking hazard.

Serves 40

Light green rolled fondant
Medium green rolled fondant
Dark green rolled fondant
Hand-modeled structure pieces (page 44)
Hand-modeled slingshot (page 44)
Hand-modeled birds (page 30)
Hand-modeled pigs (page 37)
Piping gel
Buttercream frosting
Mini pizza cutter
Flexible fondant blade
Pastry brush
14" (35.6 cm) cake board
10" (25.4 cm) round cake pan
10" (25.4 cm) plastic board or greaseproof cardboard

1. Cover the 14" (35.6 cm) cake board with light green rolled fondant.

2. Build the structures, using toothpicks to secure. Arrange the structures, slingshot, birds, and pigs on the cake. Attach the pieces using piping gel. Use a toothpick to secure the bird on top of the slingshot and the pig on top of the structure.

3. Bake and cool two single layer 10" (25.4 cm) cakes. Sandwich the two single layer cakes using buttercream. Place the cake on a 10" (25.4 cm) cardboard. Ice the cake in buttercream. Cover the cake with light green rolled fondant. Transfer the cake to the 14" (35.6 cm) covered base board.

4. Knead and soften medium green rolled fondant. Roll a 38" x 4" (96.5 x 10.2 cm) strip of fondant. Using a mini pizza cutter, cut one side of the strip in a straight line. Cut the other side of the strip with an irregular wave shape using a fondant blade.

5. Turn the strip over and brush piping gel on the back. Attach the fondant strip to the cake, placing the straight edge around the base of the cake.

6. Knead and soften medium and dark green rolled fondant. Roll the fondant into a ball. Flatten the ball. Cut the flattened fondant pieces to create grass blades. Shape the blades to create movement. Attach the grass to the cake with piping gel.

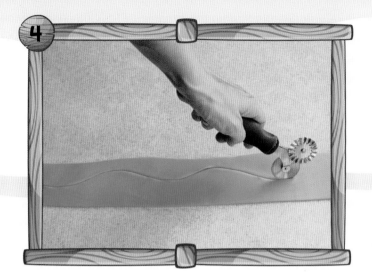

TNT Blocks with Red

Red is ready to take out structures and pigs with his TNT crates. Treat this cake as a tiered cake, using dowels to support the top TNT crate and Red. For best results, use 5" (12.7 cm) square pans with sharp corners instead of rounded corners. Slabs of textured fondant are placed on the sides of the cake.

Serves 28

- Light green rolled fondant
- Ivory rolled fondant
- White rolled fondant
- Red rolled fondant
- Burgundy rolled fondant
- Black rolled fondant
- Orange rolled fondant
- Buttercream frosting
- Brown food coloring gel
- Piping gel
- Red gum paste
- White gum paste
- Solid vegetable shortening
- Wood grain texture mat
- Flexible fondant blade
- Pastry brush
- "T" letter cutter
- "N" letter cutter
- Round cutter, 15 mm
- Round cutter, 40 mm
- Round cutter, 112 mm
- Oval cutter, 26 mm x 22 mm
- Oval cutter, 35 mm x 25 mm
- Oval cutter, 48 mm x 38 mm
- 10 x 14" cake board
- 3" (7.5 cm) round cake board
- 2 ½" (6.4 cm) round cake board
- 5" (12.7 cm) square cake pans
- 5" (12.7 cm) half sphere cake pans
- Three 5" (12.7 cm) square greaseproof cardboards
- Dowels

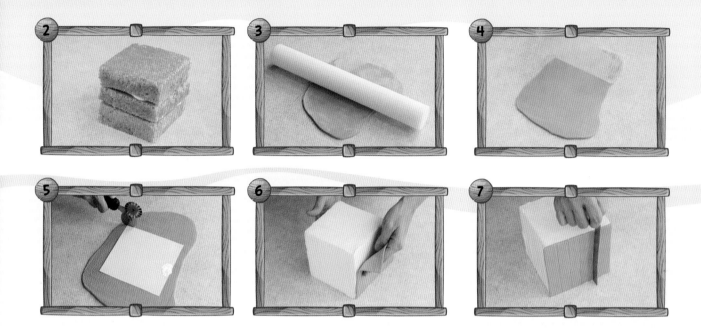

1. Cover the 3" (7.5 cm) round cake board with light green rolled fondant.

2. Bake and cool nine single layer 5" (12.7 cm) square cakes. Level each cake to be 1½" (3.8 cm) tall. Sandwich three single layer cakes using buttercream frosting. Repeat, so there are three 5" x 4½" (12.7 x 11.4 cm) three-tiered cakes. Place the cakes on 5" (12.7 cm) square cardboards. Ice each cake with buttercream.

3. Measure the height and width of one side of the cake. Create a pattern to fit the width and height of the cake. Knead and soften ivory rolled fondant. Roll the fondant 4 mm thick. Place the clean side of the rolled fondant face down onto a wood grain texture mat. Start at one end and roll over the fondant with a lot of pressure. Do not roll back and forth, or double lines will be produced. Note: When texturing the fondant, be sure to use the side of the wood grain mat that will indent the fondant, and not the side that will give a raised impression.

4. Peel back the mat. If the mat sticks, rub a bit of powdered sugar on the mat and try again.

5. Cut around the pattern with the fondant blade to cut a slab for one side of the TNT crate.

6. Place the slab on the cake. If the buttercream has crusted, brush piping gel on the back of the slab before attaching. When placing the slab on the cake, make sure the lines of the wood grain are perpendicular with the work surface.

7. Emboss wood plank lines using the fondant blade.

8. Repeat steps 4 to 7 to cover all the sides of each crate with the wood texture slabs.

(continued)

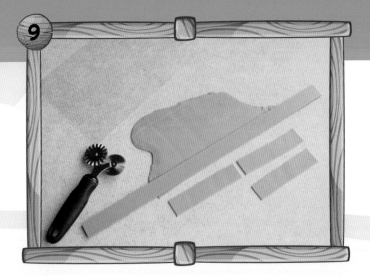

9. Knead and soften ivory rolled fondant. Roll the fondant 2 mm thick. Place the clean side of the rolled fondant face down onto the wood grain texture mat. Start at one end and roll over the fondant with a lot of pressure. Do not roll back and forth, or double lines will be produced. Note: When texturing the fondant, be sure to use the side of the wood grain mat that will indent the fondant, and not the side that will give a raised impression. Cut two strips that are ½" x 5" (1.3 x 12.7 cm). Cut two strips 3" x ½" (7.5 x 1.3 cm). Place the longer strips along the edge of the top and bottom of the crate. Place the shorter strips in between the longer strips. Note: Because the actual dimension of your baked and iced cake may vary slightly, the lengths needed may need to be a tad shorter or longer.

10. Mix brown food coloring gel with water so that the brown gel is the consistency of a watercolor paint. Brush the sides of the crate with the brown "paint" using a pastry brush.

11. Immediately wipe off the excess color using a damp paper towel. The majority of the color will be wiped off, leaving color in the indents of the wood grain texture.

12. Knead and soften white rolled fondant. Roll gum paste thin. Cut 12 white rectangles 1¼" x 2½" (3.2 x 6.4 cm).

13. Knead and soften red rolled fondant. Roll gum paste thin (#5 on a pasta machine). Rub the work surface with a thin layer of solid vegetable shortening. The shortening should not be visible. Place the rolled fondant on the shortening-covered countertop. Cut 24 Ts and 12 Ns using the letter cutters.

14. Pull away the excess fondant.

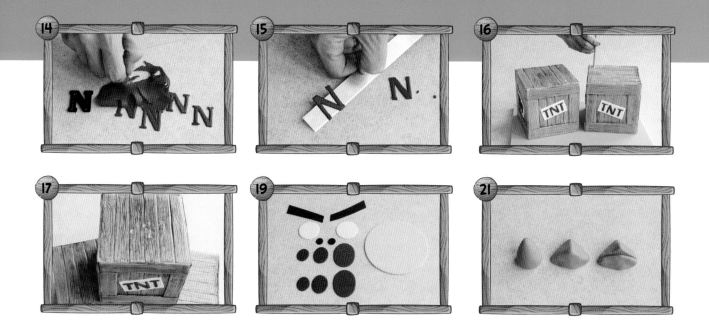

15. Allow the letters to harden for a few minutes. If the cutters have a serif (as these cutters do), cut off the serif. When the letters have hardened, carefully slide the fondant blade under the letter to release from the work surface. Attach the letters to the white rectangle. Place the TNT labels on each side of the block using piping gel to attach.

16. Position two of the TNT crates on the 3" (7.5 cm) cake board, using buttercream icing underneath each block to secure the cakes to the board. Insert two dowels into each cake, approximately 1" (2.5 cm) from the closest edge to the center. The dowels should be the height of the cake and rest on the board. These dowels are used to keep the third TNT crate from crushing the first and second crates. Place the third crate on top, using buttercream icing to secure the third crate to the bottom two.

17. Insert three dowels into the center of the third crate. The dowels should be the height of the cake and rest on the third crate's cardboard. These dowels are used to keep Red from sinking into the third crate.

18. Bake and cool two 5" (12.7 cm) half sphere cakes following the baking instructions on page 18. Ice each cake with buttercream and adhere together following the icing instructions on pages 19-20. Place the sphere cake on a 2 ½" (6.4 cm) round cake board.

Cover the cake with red rolled fondant following the instructions on page 20.

19. Knead and soften ivory rolled fondant. Roll thin. Cut a circle using the 112 mm round cutter. Knead and soften burgundy rolled fondant. Roll thin. Using the oval cutters, cut burgundy ovals, cutting two of each size. Knead and soften white rolled fondant. Roll thin. Cut two circles using the 40 mm round cutter. Knead and soften black rolled fondant. Roll thin. Cut two circles using the 15 mm round cutter. Attach the black pupils to the white eyes using piping gel. Cut the top one-fifth off the eyes. Knead and soften black rolled fondant. Roll thin. Cut the eyebrows using the flexible fondant blade. Place the face accents on the bird's body using piping gel to attach.

20. Knead and soften red rolled fondant. Roll two teardrops for Red's head comb, making one a little larger than the other.

21. Knead and soften orange rolled fondant. Form a cone for the beak. Shape the cone into a triangle. Use the flexible fondant blade to cut the beak.

22. Center Red on top of the third crate, using buttercream icing to secure Red to the crate.

Birdday Party Tiered Cake

Serves 50

White rolled fondant
Blue rolled fondant
Yellow rolled fondant
Burgundy rolled fondant
Pink rolled fondant
Orange rolled fondant
Light green rolled fondant
Light blue rolled fondant
Light yellow rolled fondant
Brown rolled fondant
Light mauve rolled fondant
Mauve rolled fondant
Dark mauve rolled fondant
Red rolled fondant
Hot pink rolled fondant
Hand-modeled birds (page 30)
Hand-modeled pigs (page 37)
Hand-modeled structures
   (page 44)
Piping gel
Black food coloring pen
Brown food coloring pen
Buttercream frosting
Mini triangle cutter
Round cutter, 2" (5 cm)
Round cutter, 4" (10.2 cm)
Round cutter, 30 mm
Flexible fondant blade
Mini pizza cutter
White-covered wire, 22 gauge
Pastry bag
Tip #2A
Pastry brush
Fondant extruder
18" (45.7 cm) round cake board
7" (17.8 cm) round cake pan
12" (30.5 cm) round cake pan
9" (23 cm) square cake pan
Standard cupcake pan
7" (17.8 cm) greaseproof
   cardboard or cake plate
12" (30.5 cm) greaseproof
   cardboard or cake plate

This cake was inspired by the Birdday level. Nearly every popular character is represented on this cake, and some of the Angry Birds even have adorable birthday hats atop their heads. This cake is perhaps the most time-consuming of all the cakes. Allow ample time to complete the cake, making all of the characters and the structures several days ahead of time.

1. Form cones for the party hats using white rolled fondant and blue rolled fondant. Cut strips of white, yellow, and mauve rolled fondant for the stripes on the white hat. Attach with piping gel. Roll a ball of yellow fondant for the top of the hat, attaching with piping gel. Place the striped hat on Terence's head. Roll various sizes of tiny balls using pink fondant for the dots on the blue hat. Attach with piping gel. Roll a ball of pink fondant for the top of the hat, attaching with piping gel. Place the blue hat on Hal.

2. Roll orange fondant thin. Cut a strip of orange fondant. Use a mini triangle cutter to cut the zigzag pattern for Matilda's crown. Roll white fondant thin. Cut a triangle. Cut a strip. Fold the strip and allow to harden. When hard, use a black food marker to color the details. Place the hat on Bomb's head.

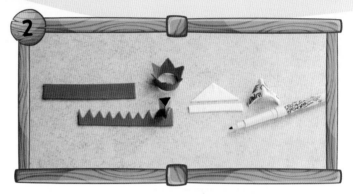

3. Knead and soften yellow rolled fondant. Form an egg shape for the balloon. Form a small triangle for the balloon tie. Color a white covered wire with a brown food color marker. Attach the balloon to the wire using piping gel to adhere. Allow the balloon to harden overnight.

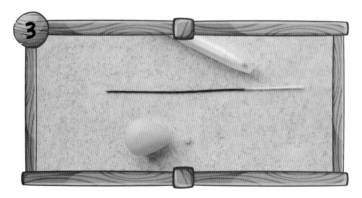

4. Cover the 18" (45.7 cm) cake board with light green rolled fondant.

5. Bake and cool two single layer 7" (17.8 cm) cakes. Sandwich the two single layer cakes using buttercream. Place the cake on a 7" (17.8 cm) cardboard. Ice the cake in buttercream. Cover the cake with light blue rolled fondant.

6. Bake and cool two single layer 12" (30.5 cm) cakes. Sandwich the two single layer cakes using buttercream. Place the cake on a 12" (30.5 cm) cardboard. Ice the cake in buttercream. Cover the cake with light blue rolled fondant.

7. Bake and cool a 9" (23 cm) square cake. When cool, cut a 2" (5 cm) circle and a 4" (10.2 cm) circle using round cutters.

(continued)

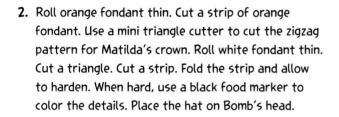

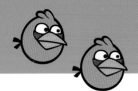

8. Layer the mini cake, using buttercream icing in between the layers.

9. Fill a pastry bag with buttercream icing and tip #2A. Pipe rings around the cake.

10. Smooth the buttercream with a spatula. Cover the mini tier cake with light yellow rolled fondant.

11. Bake a cupcake. Allow the cupcake to cool. Cut off the top of the cupcake so the top is straight instead of domed.

12. Remove the cupcake paper. Turn the cupcake over. Brush piping gel on the cupcake. Knead and soften brown rolled fondant. Roll thin and cover the cupcake with brown rolled fondant. Cut around the base. Turn the cupcake back over. Brush piping gel on the top of the cupcake. Roll brown fondant thin. Cut a round disk of brown rolled fondant. Set the circle on the cupcake.

13. Cut apart the pattern for the Birdday background on page 93. Knead and soften light mauve rolled fondant. Roll thin. Place the pattern on the rolled fondant. Cut around the pattern using a cutting blade. Brush piping gel on the back of the cut background. Place on the cake. Repeat with the medium pattern using mauve rolled fondant and the small pattern using dark mauve rolled fondant. Layer the backgrounds.

14. Knead and soften red rolled fondant. Cut a circle for the cherry using the 30 mm round cutter. Cut the edges using a fondant blade, if necessary, to fit among the mauve background. Knead and soften brown rolled fondant. Roll a cherry stem. Attach the cherries and the stems to the cake with piping gel.

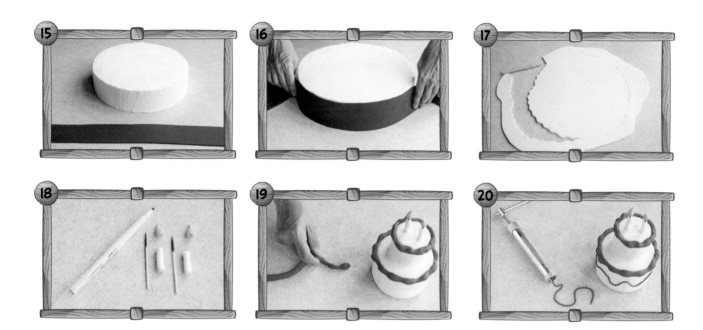

15. Knead and soften burgundy rolled fondant. Roll a 38" (96.5 cm) long strip. Using a mini pizza cutter, cut the strip so that it is exactly the height of the cake. Carefully turn over the strip. Brush piping gel on the back of the strip.

16. Start by lifting the strip in the center and attach the fondant strip to the cake. Gently press to attach the strip to the cake.

17. Knead and soften white rolled fondant. Emboss the fondant with a 12" (30.5 cm) cake pan to create a circle outline. Cut a wavy outline using the embossed circle as the guideline, cutting just outside the embossed circle. Brush piping gel on top of the 12" (30.5 cm) cake. Place the cut 12" (30.5 cm) wavy circle on top of the cake.

18. Color the end of a toothpick black. Knead and soften yellow rolled fondant. Shape two teardrops. Knead and soften white rolled fondant. Roll two snakes. Cut the ends with a fondant blade to create a sharp edge. Place the white snakes and teardrops on the toothpicks for the candles.

19. Knead and soften hot pink rolled fondant. Roll a long snake with even thickness. Use your finger and thumb to give the snake a wavy shape. Use piping gel to attach the snake to the mini tier cake.

20. Knead and soften hot pink rolled fondant. Feed the rolled fondant into the extruder with a small circle attached. Pipe a line of piping gel onto the mini tier cake where the string will be placed. Attach the string to the cake.

21. Transfer the 12" (30.5 cm) cake to the 18" (45.7 cm) covered base board, placing the cake toward the back of the board. Stack the 7" (17.8 cm) cake on top of the 12" (30.5 cm) cake, placing the 7" (17.8 cm) cake toward the back of the 12" (30.5 cm) cake. Place the mini tier cake on top of the 12" (30.5 cm) cake. Place the brown fondant-covered cupcake on the blue top tier.

22. Arrange the Angry Birds, Bad Piggies, and structures on the cake, using toothpicks to secure their position. Do not cut the toothpicks. If the pieces are too short for a standard size toothpick, simply attach to the board or cake with piping gel.

Cake Pops

Cake pops are a terrific accent to cakes and cupcakes. They are also a wonderful take-home party favor. Cake pops are made by taking a baked cake, crumbling the cake, then mixing the cake with a small amount of icing so that it makes a dough consistency that can be shaped. This section covers the basics for making the cake pops. Then use the tools and instructions on hand molding (pages 30-43) to create the character details.

General Instructions

Cake pops are tasty and adorable, but they can be time-consuming. Save time on the day the cake pops will be made by making the accents, such as the eyes, beak, and eyebrows up to several weeks ahead of time. If making the accents ahead of time, create a "dummy body" by forming the shape of the body with rolled fondant to test and ensure all of the features will be proportional. Cake pops are best eaten within four or five days.

Mixing the baked cake with icing is easiest simply by using your hands. It's also a great way to involve kids. Allow the kids to crumble the cake mixture with their hands. Then, add the icing and blend with their hands. If this doesn't sound appealing, a fork can be used to crumble the cake. Use the back of a large spoon to blend the icing.

The amount of icing used is one of the most important factors for success in making cake pops. The amount given is a suggestion, but more or less icing may be needed. Extra-moist cake requires very little icing, while cakes that are drier require a little more icing. The type of icing used will also affect the consistency of the cake pop mixture. Buttercream icing is used for the cake pops in this book, but grocery store icing can also be used. The grocery store icing is thinner, so less of this icing will be needed.

One cake mix will make 18 to 24 cake pops sized 1" to 1 1/2" (2.5 to 3.8 cm). Although King Pig and Foreman Pig are proportionally larger than the rest of the birds, it is important when making cake pops to scale their size down closer to the birds' size. Cake pops larger than 2" (5 cm) will likely be too heavy for the stick.

CANDY COATING

Candy coating, often called almond bark, candy wafers, compound coating, or Candy Melts, is a chocolate-like product that is perfect for dipping cake pops. The coating is available in milk, dark, or white chocolate. It is also available in a rainbow of colors, which are ideal to use for the birds. Some candy color may be needed to achieve the birds' colors. When adding candy color, it is important to use an oil-based coloring. Other food colors contain water, which may thicken the coating. Use the following suggestions to obtain the colors of melted candy coating of the birds.

Red: Red candy coating with a few drops of pink candy color to brighten the red

Chuck: Yellow candy coating with a few drops of yellow candy color and one drop of orange candy color

Matilda: Super white candy coating

Bomb: Black candy coating

The Blues: Blue candy coating

Hal: Green candy coating

Bad Piggies: Yellow candy coating with a few drops of yellow and one or two drops of green candy color

Note: Candy coatings vary in viscosity. Paramount crystals (available at cake and candy supply stores) or 1 to 2 tablespoons (15 to 30 ml) of vegetable oil can be added to thin the candy coating.

MAKING CAKE POPS

1. Bake and cool any flavor of cake. Place the baked and cooled cake in a bowl. Crumble the cake with your hands until the cake is coarse crumbs.

2. Add a small amount of icing (start with 1 tablespoon [15 g]). Blend the icing in with your hands. The amount of icing needed will vary depending on the moistness of the cake. Typically only 1 or 2 tablespoons

(15 to 30 g) of icing may be needed. Add just enough icing so that the cake holds together when squeezed in your hand without being sticky.

3. Remove a spoonful of the cake pop mixture. A cookie scoop can be used for uniform size.

4. Roll the cake pop into a ball, an egg shape, or a triangle, depending on the desired bird. Place the cake pops into the freezer for 15 minutes to firm.

   The Blues: 1" (2.5 cm) ball (A)

   Red: 1 1/4" (3.1 cm) ball (B)

   Bomb: 1 1/2" (3.8 cm) ball (C)

   Hal: 1 1/4" (3.1 cm) ball (C)

   Matilda: 1 1/2" (3.8 cm) ball, then form into an egg (D)

   Chuck: 1 1/4" (3.1 cm) ball, then form into a triangle (E)

   Bad Piggies: 1 1/4" (3.1 cm) for the Minion Pigs (B) and 1 1/2" (3.8 cm) for King Pig and Foreman Pig (F)

5. Place candy coating in a microwave-safe bowl. Heat the candy coating in the microwave for 30 seconds. Stir. Heat the candy coating for 10 more seconds. Continue heating in 10-second intervals until the candy coating is smooth. Dip the end of the sucker stick into the melted candy coating. Immediately poke the stick halfway into a chilled cake pop. Allow the coating to set for a few minutes.

6. After a few minutes, spoon melted candy coating onto the cake pop. Rotate the stick to ensure the pop is completely coated. Hold the pop over

the melted candy coating bowl and rotate the stick, allowing excess candy coating to drip off the pop. Continue rotating the stick until the candy coating on the pop is nearly set.

7. When the candy coating is nearly set and no longer dripping, insert the cake pop on a stick into a block of Styrofoam to continue to firm up.

DECORATING THE CAKE POPS

Tools Used

Some of the shapes used on the bird and pig cake pops are hand molded, such as the beak and the pigs' noses. To create accents for the cake pops, use the tools and instructions for hand modeling fondant (page 30-43). A flexible fondant blade is ideal to cut the eyebrows and the head feathers of the birds. Circle cutters in a variety of sizes are useful for the eyes and contrasting belly. Mini accent cutters are perfect for cutting small facial accents on the Angry Birds and Bad Piggies. A ball tool is used for the nostrils and ears on the pigs. Black nonpareils are used for the pupils on most of the characters. The accents are attached to the cake pop using piping gel.

When cake pops are made to accompany other projects, such as the cakes or cupcakes in this book, rolled fondant is ideal for the accents on the cake pops because there may be unused rolled fondant left over from the cake or cupcake projects. It is important to keep the rolled fondant accents thin (other than the beaks) so the texture does not overpower the texture of the cake pop. The cake pops in this book were decorated using rolled fondant.

An alternative to rolled fondant is candy fondant. To mix candy fondant, simply stir $1/3$ cup (80 ml) of corn syrup into a $1/2$ pound (226 g) of melted colored candy coating. The mixture will immediately become stiff and will thicken to a fudgelike consistency. Pour the mixture onto a piece of plastic wrap. Wrap the candy fondant tightly. Allow the candy fondant to set for several hours before using.

Tip!

- When blending the baked cake with the icing, add a spoonful of icing at a time.
- When forming shapes with the cake pop mixture, the mixture should not be crumbly or sticky. If it crumbles when rolled, add more icing. If it is sticky, add more cake.
- If the pop is falling off the stick when dipping, the candy coating on the sucker stick may not have had enough time to firm up, or the stick may have been inserted too far into the pop.
- If the shell cracks after being dipped into the candy coating, the cake pop may be too cold. Allow the cake pop to come nearly to room temperature before dipping into the candy coating. The cake pop should be slightly cool, but not frozen. Usually dipping the stick into the melted candy coating as soon as the cake pop comes out of the freezer, then allowing the candy coating to set, is enough time to eliminate the cracking. If there is still cracking, the cake pop can be dipped a second time.
- If the candy coating seems thick when dipping, paramount crystals or vegetable oil can be added to thin the candy.
- Candy coating is easily scorched. When it is overheated, it thickens. Melt slowly in the microwave, and always stir between intervals. Stop melting when there are just a few unmelted wafers left. Then stir until the coating is smooth.
- Water will thicken the candy coating. Make sure your hands are thoroughly dry before working with the candy coating. Do not use any water-based food coloring to color the candy coating.
- If candy coating has dripped down the sucker stick, use a paring knife to scrape off excess candy from the stick.
- Dark cakes, such as chocolate, may show through after the cake pop is dipped. The cake pop can be double-dipped, or use a light-colored cake such as white or yellow.

Many Expressions

RED

CHUCK

MATILDA

BOMB

HAL

BLUE   KING PIG   FOREMAN PIG

MINION PIGS

Cupcakes

This section includes designs for 20 different Angry Birds cupcakes. We'll start with the basics for baking, icing, and covering a cupcake with rolled fondant. Then, use the photographs for inspiration and follow the instructions to make a fabulous array of crowd-pleasing cupcakes.

General Instructions

BAKING CUPCAKES

1. Line a cupcake pan with baking cups. Follow the recipe's instructions for mixing the cake batter. Use an ice cream scoop to fill the baking cups. The cups should be a little over half full. If making Chuck cupcakes, create a triangle by placing foil to shape the cup before baking.

2. Place the filled cupcake pan in the oven and bake according to the recipe's instructions. After the cupcakes are baked, remove the pan from the oven and place on a cooling rack. Allow the pan to cool for 10 minutes, then remove the cupcakes and place them on a cooling rack. Allow the cupcakes to cool completely before decorating, or the icing will melt.

COVERING A CUPCAKE WITH ROLLED FONDANT

1. Ice the cupcake with buttercream icing. It's best to use the same color of icing as the fondant disk so if any icing leaks, it will not be noticeable.

2. Knead and soften rolled fondant. Roll to 2 mm thick. Cut a circle using a 75 mm round cutter. Place the circle on the cupcake.

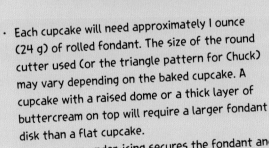

3. Use a fondant smoother to gently smooth and round the top of the cupcake.

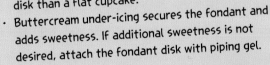

PIPING ICING ON A CUPCAKE

1. Fit a pastry bag using a tip with a large opening. Tips #IA, #IM, and #8B are nice tips for piping icing onto cupcakes. Fill the pastry bag with buttercream icing. Pipe a dot in the center of the cupcake.

2. Pipe a ring around the dot, then continue piping around the cupcake, spiraling until the desired size.

Tip!

- Each cupcake will need approximately I ounce (24 g) of rolled fondant. The size of the round cutter used (or the triangle pattern for Chuck) may vary depending on the baked cupcake. A cupcake with a raised dome or a thick layer of buttercream on top will require a larger fondant disk than a flat cupcake.
- Buttercream under-icing secures the fondant and adds sweetness. If additional sweetness is not desired, attach the fondant disk with piping gel.

Angry Birds Scene Cupcakes

These cupcakes covered with fondant are like mini scenes taken right out of the game. Mold your favorite birds and piggies using the instructions on pages 30-43, then cut gum paste bushes and cacti using a knife and the patterns on page 92. The bushes and cacti should be made ahead of time to allow ample time to firm. Elements that need extra support can be propped with a full-length toothpick (a short toothpick is a choking hazard) and be sure to remove the toothpick before serving. Use piping gel to secure the characters and props to the cupcakes.

Indent the fondant to keep the bird or piggy from falling off the cupcake.

Angry Birds Face Cupcakes

These cupcakes are covered with fondant and the facial features are hand molded or cut using a flexible fondant blade and various sizes of round and oval cutters. Use a full-length toothpick to prop extending elements, such as Bomb's head feather, and be sure to remove the toothpick before serving. Use the pattern on page 93 to cut the fondant top for Chuck's cupcake.

RED   CHUCK   BOMB

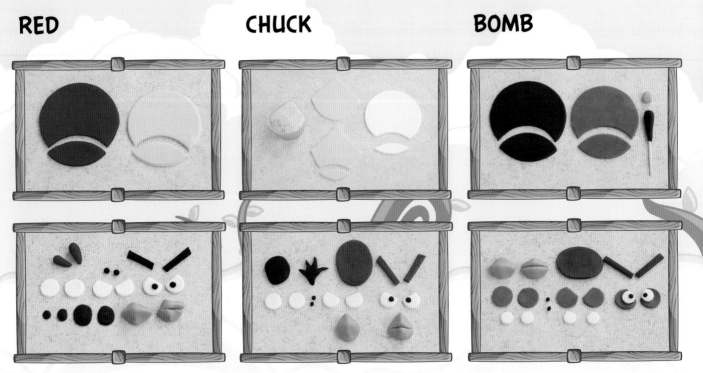

MINION PIG

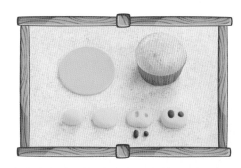
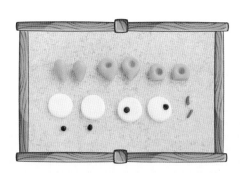

NEST

Dark ivory buttercream
Dark ivory rolled fondant
Jordon almonds
Pastry bag
Tip #IA
Fondant extruder

1. Fit a pastry bag with tip #IA. Pipe ivory icing onto the cupcake and spread smooth. Pipe an additional band of icing around the edge of the cupcake.

2. Knead and soften dark ivory fondant. Form a snake. Feed the snake into the extruder barrel and pipe onto the cupcake in a nest formation. Place Jordan almonds in the center of the nest.

Angry Birds Plaques

These cupcakes are piped with a mound of buttercream, then a disk of fondant adds the Angry Birds theme. The disks need a couple of days to harden to ensure they stand up on the cupcakes, and they can be created several weeks ahead, making these cupcakes ideal time-savers on party day. Make all the light blue plaques first, using a 56 mm cutter. Then create several plaques of each character assembly style, using a flexible fondant blade and various sizes of round and oval cutters.

RED

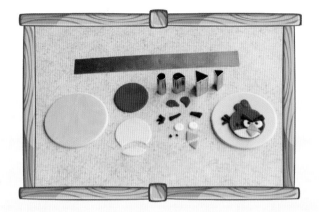

MATILDA

CHUCK

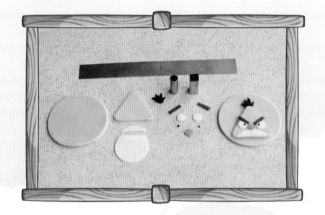

MINION PIG

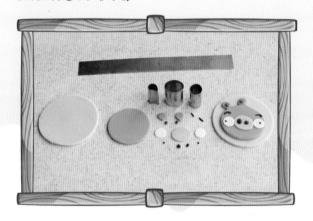

BOMB

Patterns

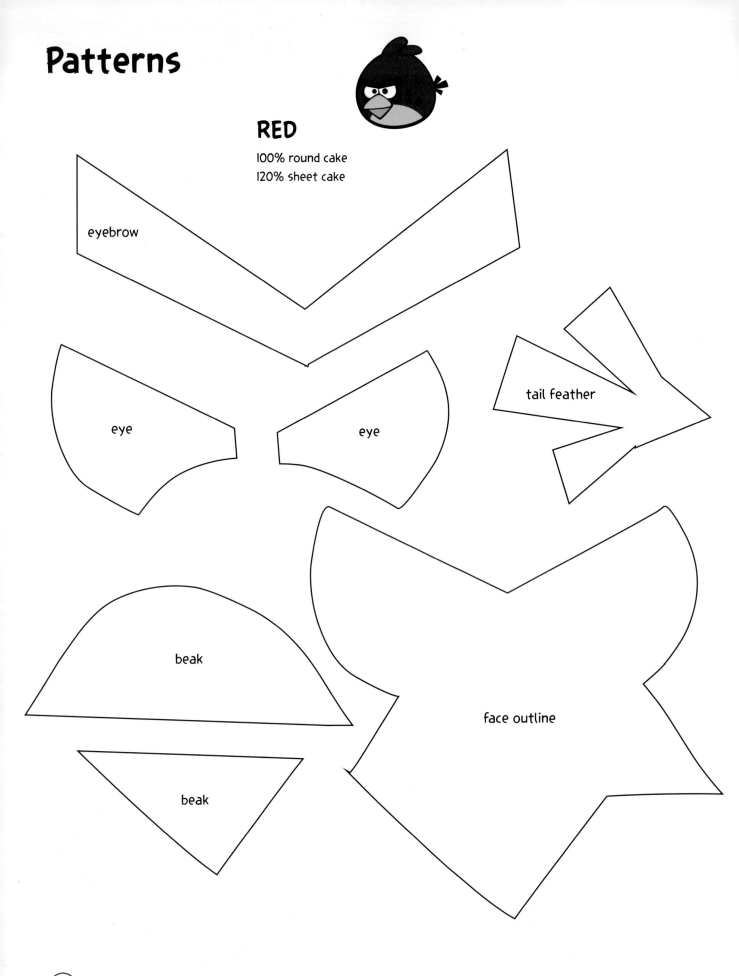

RED

100% round cake
120% sheet cake

eyebrow

eye

eye

tail feather

beak

beak

face outline

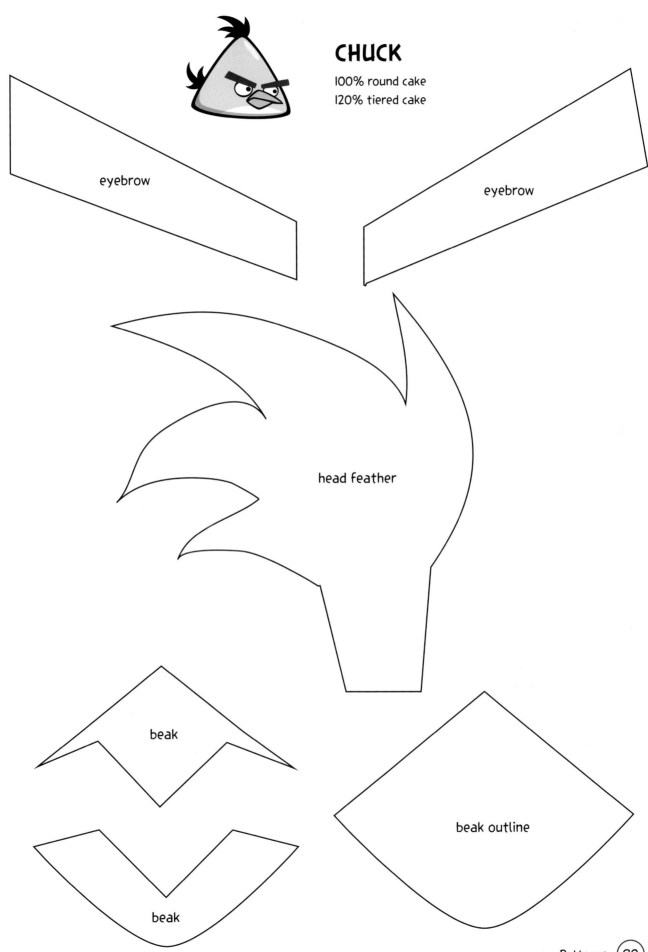

CHUCK

100% round cake
120% tiered cake

eyebrow

eyebrow

head feather

beak

beak

beak outline

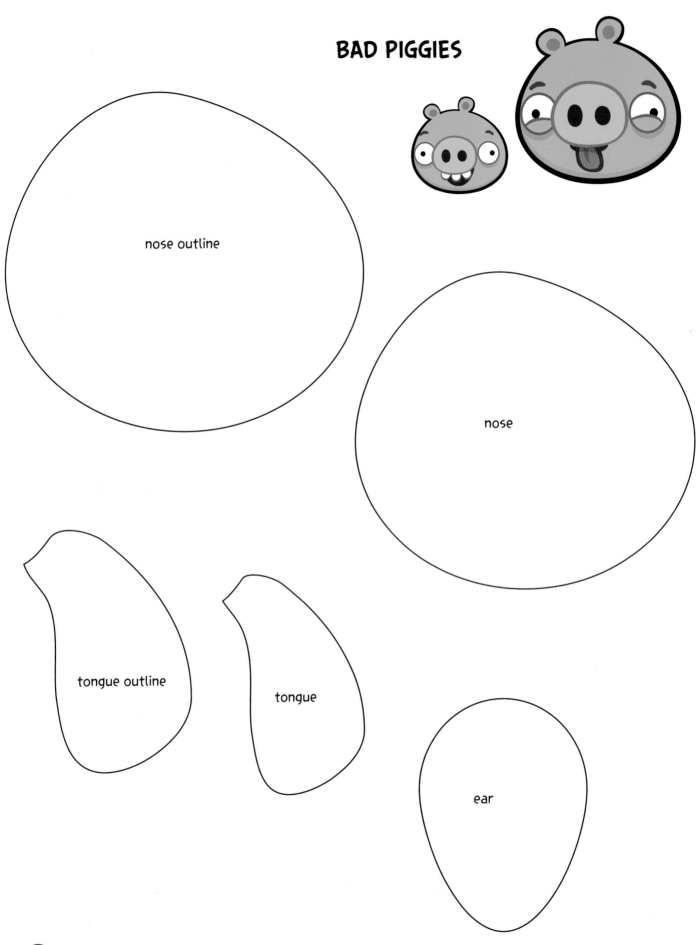

BAD PIGGIES

nose outline

nose

tongue outline

tongue

ear

THE BLUES

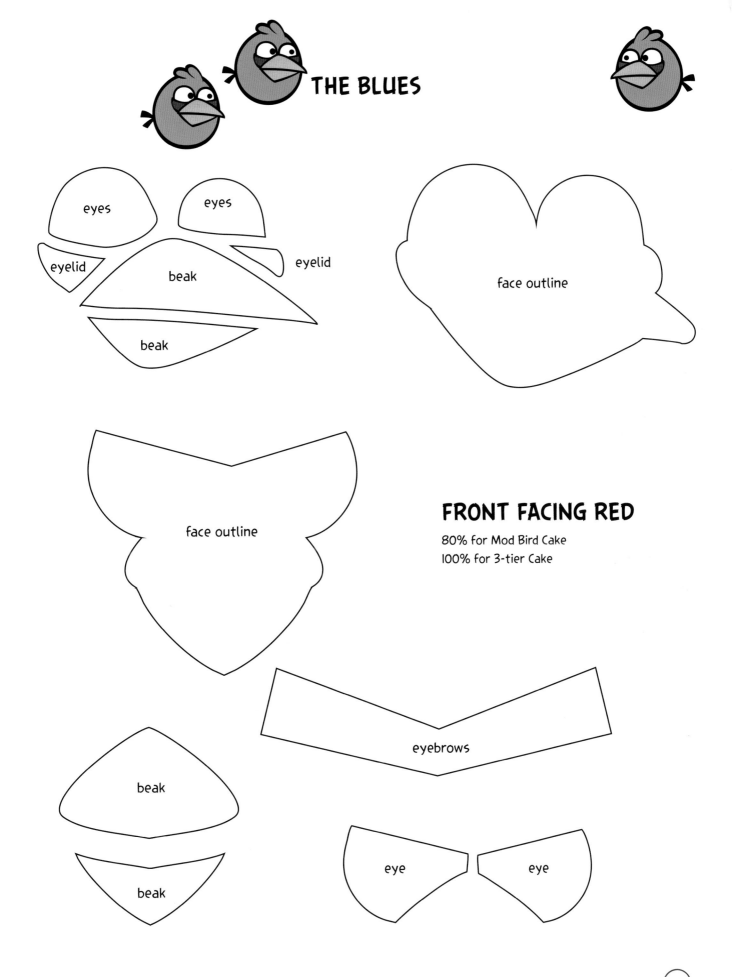

eyes

eyes

eyelid

eyelid

beak

beak

face outline

face outline

FRONT FACING RED

80% for Mod Bird Cake
100% for 3-tier Cake

eyebrows

beak

beak

eye

eye

SQUARE MOD CAKE

Blue ray

SCENE CUPCAKES

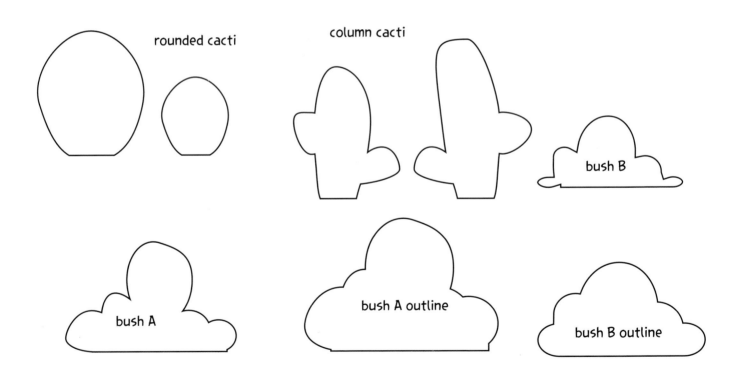

rounded cacti

column cacti

bush B

bush A

bush A outline

bush B outline

Let's Make Angry Birds Cakes

CHUCK CUPCAKE

BIRDDAY PARTY

Autumn Carpenter Designs

Mini accent cutters, perfection strips, texture mats.

Blog

www.autumncarpenter.wordpress.com

Country Kitchen SweetArt

A one-stop shop carrying the cake and candy
supplies used throughout the book.
www.shopcountrykitchen.com

Sweet Elite Tools

Cutters, texture mats.
www.sweetelitetools.com

Websites

www.autumncarpenter.com
www.cookiedecorating.com

Autumn Carpenter's passion for decorating started at a very young age. Growing up in the confectionary industry, Autumn found joy in every aspect of the business. Autumn is co-owner of Country Kitchen SweetArt, a retail cake and candy supply store that has been owned and operated within Autumn's family for more than 45 years. The business caters to walk-in store sales, catalog sales, and online sales at www.shopcountrykitchen.com.

Autumn has demonstrated her techniques throughout the country, teaches on Craftsy.com, and serves as a judge in cake decorating competitions. She has been a member, teacher, and demonstrator at the International Cake Exploration Society (ICES) for 20 years.

Autumn's own line of useful tools and equipment for cake and cookie decorating can be found online as well as in many cake and candy supply stores throughout the United States and in several countries. She has written several books, including *The Complete Photo Guide to Cake Decorating*; *The Complete Photo Guide to Cookie Decorating*; *The Complete Photo Guide to Candy Making*; and *Decorate Cakes, Cupcakes, and Cookies with Kids*.

Acknowledgments

Thanks once again to my editor, Linda Neubauer, for giving me an opportunity to write a fifth book! Special thanks to Ryan, the sweet six-year-old who made sure I was well informed on every detail of the Angry Birds, Minion Pigs, and all the levels of the game. Above all, I want to thank my husband and my kids, who supported and encouraged me in spite of all the time it took me away from them.